"*Buoyant* is a map for entrepreneurs and creators who crave success and freedom. In this transformational book, Susie deVille helps you get out of stuck and self-doubt and find flow, ease, and joy by reclaiming inspired creativity and aligning with your true self."

JONATHAN FIELDS, founder, Good Life Project® and Spark Endeavors; author of *Sparked: Discover Your Unique Imprint for Work That Makes You Come Alive*

"Free-flowing creativity and authenticity are a powerful duo. Susie deVille shows you how to become the most powerful version of yourself by unlocking both in her generous book, *Buoyant*. A wonderful read for entrepreneurs ready to welcome their next level."

SUSIE MOORE, bestselling author of *Let It Be Easy*

"*Buoyant* is exactly what a creative thinker needs to help them gain control of their journey and get back on track."

SYLVIA WEHRLE, creative director experience, Publicis Sapient

"When entrepreneurs want to grow, they often think they have to work harder and faster which leads to burnout and depletion. Susie deVille, in her brilliant and inspiring book *Buoyant*, shows another way: by understanding our unique voice and vision and tapping the natural patterns of our creativity, we generate sustained energy, strategic clarity, and ease while we grow."

PAMELA SLIM, author of *The Widest Net* and *Body of Work*

"A supportive and reflective guide for entrepreneurs to help release the creativity that has been hiding inside of us."

SUSAN M. BARBER, executive coach; author of *The Visibility Factor*

"Amidst a sea of business books that promise to help us correct some aspect of ourselves, *Buoyant* is a magical must-read that helps us embrace our whole selves and reconnect with the creative spark that inspired us to become entrepreneurs. Each chapter offers a delicious experience that helps us tap into desires long dormant and open doors long shut."

AJ HARPER, author of *Write a Must-Read*

"*Buoyant* demonstrates how to break through stuckness using creativity as the overarching tool. But don't be intimidated by the limiting belief that you may not be creative. There are doable exercises to walk you through the process."

LORI PETERSEN, CEO and founder, AccountSolve, LLC

"*Buoyant* guides us into a consciousness of appreciation—greater appreciation results in greater creativity, no matter the application—and takes us into a new understanding of ourselves."

KNIGHT MARTORELL, founder and CEO, Martorell Studios

"This book is part inspiration, part road map to help you reconnect with your true self so you can live more authentically."

CYNDI THOMASON, author and speaker;
founder and president, bookskeep

"*Buoyant* takes us on an adventure of personal and professional growth through Susie deVille's unique methodology of using creativity as a magical tool."

GABI DALNEKOFF, CEO and founder, AweVida

"Part autobiography of a successful entrepreneur, part how-to on finding and reconnecting with your soul, *Buoyant* is a book that you'll have a hard time putting down."

RACHEL GOGOS, founder and CEO, brandiD

BUOYANT

The Entrepreneur's Guide to Becoming Wildly Successful, Creative, and Free

Susie deVille

Buoyant

PAGE TWO

Cataloguing in publication information is available
from Library and Archives Canada.
ISBN 978-1-77458-181-0 (paperback)
ISBN 978-1-77458-182-7 (ebook)
ISBN 978-1-77458-283-1 (audiobook)

Page Two
pagetwo.com

Edited by Amanda Lewis and Scott Steedman
Copyedited by Steph VanderMeulen
Proofread by Alison Strobel
Cover and interior design by Taysia Louie
Interior illustrations by Michelle Clement
Elephant illustration on pp. 87 and 88
by Knight Martorell and Michelle Clement
Printed and bound in Canada by Friesens
Distributed in Canada by Raincoast Books
Distributed in the US and internationally by Macmillan

22 23 24 25 26   5 4 3 2 1

InnovationandCreativityInstitute.com

For Adam

Contents

Introduction

I F YOU are on the floor right now, I know just how frightened you are.

My moment on the floor began in 2008, when the financial markets crashed. The dominoes that had been teetering for years—my business, my marriage, my finances, my health, my joy in living, my sense of self—didn't just fall, they came crashing down on my head as if they had been carelessly stored in a forgotten shoebox on the edge of a closet shelf.

Two hundred and fifty thousand dollars in debt. A house in foreclosure. A body I had neglected for years, carrying an extra seventy pounds. A business in a nosedive. A heart so shattered, I swept up the shards and dust as best I could and put the bits on ice, like you do with a severed finger. Fear that had me by the ankles—a dead weight I dragged around all day and night.

My immediate concern was addressing the challenges in my business. I needed a solid and stable place to put my feet financially so that I could make a living and dig myself out of debt. I knew that if I could connect powerfully with the clients I most wanted to serve, sales would follow. Once I had established some breathing room in my business, I reasoned,

I could turn my attention to resolving the various messes in my personal life.

So I began chasing clients. I maintained a frenetic pace, working late each evening and rising before dawn the next day to start all over again. I searched for business success magic bullets and implemented the tactics I read about in books and learned in webinars and coaching sessions.

I threw business strategy spaghetti against the wall. Nothing stuck. I began to panic even more. What I didn't realize then was that all my scurrying around, "push" marketing efforts, lack of rest, toxic thinking and habits, and relentless anxiety weren't helping—they were actually *keeping me* from success. I was miserable.

Perhaps you are in a season of gripping fear over your business right now and are confused about and stuck on how to make things better. Maybe you, like most of my entrepreneur coaching clients, feel overwhelmed, exhausted, as if you are drowning, unsure of how to extricate yourself from the chaotic spiral of pursuing success. Maybe you believe that it's not just your business that's broken—you are, too.

Let me cut to the chase and give you the first of many blasts of sweet, restorative oxygen contained in this book: You can find the way back to yourself and out of being stuck in your business. You are not broken. The prevalent advice to entrepreneurs, however, *is* broken.

The reason the things you've tried haven't worked is that the common advice given to us entrepreneurs is based on the notion that we are missing some "right" formula or key to productivity. That we need to commit, go all in. Burn the boats. Build better funnels. Dial up our efforts. We can sleep when we're dead!

Of course, dedication, strategic focus, and discipline are all important and contribute to the health of our business.

The problem is that this advice is woefully incomplete. At its best, it's not enough. At its worst, it just depletes us further by cementing us more deeply into the belief that more doing holds the answers. When we expend our energy and reorient our focus to be further outside of ourselves, we neglect to feed and water our personal reserves of creativity, the power plants of ideas, imagination, and essential intuition.

The place for conventional business advice is *after* we have done the work to ensure our inspiration buckets are filled to the brim, and we have mindfully turned over the soil of us to support sustainable creativity over the long term. Skipping the essential inspiration steps is like trying fill balloons when there is no air in our lungs.

I have a different approach, and it works.

I promise that if you take the advice in this book to heart and do the exercises, you will discover an easier path to success and freedom. I realize you may find it hard to believe at first that my methodology works. You may resist doing the exercises. I understand. I remember my own path to transformation. I would have been supremely skeptical as well.

Let's start with the basics to get our feet wet in the shallow end of the pool. Here is the foundational truth of how to change everything in your business and life: By reclaiming and reconnecting with inspiration and your innate creativity, you can bring resounding happiness back into your life and enjoy business success you thought was out of reach.

I'm going to stay here for a minute and let that sink in. I know this is hard to believe. I also know how loaded the word "creativity" is. You most likely don't consider yourself creative. I can sense you backing up, feeling around for the door handle. Your business is in dire straits, and here I am, offering you the equivalent of a glue stick and some paints as the panacea. And inspiration? What?

Please stay with me. Even if the only thing you are willing to believe right now is that what I am saying is possible, that is enough.

Another small step forward now. How does one go about reclaiming and reconnecting with inspiration and one's innate creativity?

By bringing yourself back to life.

I know—I did it. Over the course of a little more than a decade, I crafted myself, my life, and my businesses anew. I transformed my body from being dangerously overweight to being in shape and healthy. I shed my addictions to my toxic habits of choice: working fourteen-hour days and then coming home to eat and drink to distract myself from feeling. I dug out from beneath a mountain of debt, paid for my children's educations with cash, and funded my retirement.

No one was more surprised than I that the solutions I clamored for didn't turn out to be a mash-up of hustle, grind, and whipping myself onward. Nor were the answers contained in the reams of handouts I got from business webinars. Instead, turning everything around began with being kind to myself. Gentle immersion into inspiring and creative acts fueled my desire, commitment, and energy stores to transform every aspect of my businesses and life by making small changes each day.

I remembered what I loved, and what I loved to do. I began traveling again and discovered all the pleasures of adventure and its accompanying freedom. I returned to immersing myself in nature, going on long hikes with my golden retriever, Sophie, under a canopy of pines, oaks, and poplars. I began writing again after twenty years of ignoring a craft I forgot I once adored. These experiences were jolts of electricity to my flatlined soul. As I brought myself back online, little by little, I sought out more and more opportunities to beef up my joy pulse and reconnect to stimuli that fired and rewired my synapses. My energy, focus, and clarity went way up, as did my confidence and tolerance for uncertainty.

I delved into transformational learning experiences around the globe. I learned how to meditate, speak in front of groups without a script, cook and bake, grasp the basics of conversing and writing in French, walk on fire, and sail. I took a coaching certification course, leadership training, and a publicity and promotion intensive. I reworked and empowered my mindset at retreats in the United States and Europe.

I began taking sketching, painting, and mixed media classes, as well as instruction on how to draw comics. Through these courses, I discovered the biggest lies of my life: 1) the belief that I was not an artist, 2) the belief that the things we create are the point of engaging in creativity, and 3) the notion that our creative efforts must be judged as being "good" for them (and us) to have value.

Did I become a great artist? That remains to be seen and, truthfully, is irrelevant. I came away with so much more than achieving some sort of elusive, subjective status. I learned how to see, how to hone my awareness, and how to sink into a deep presence in the moment, letting my intuition come to the fore. I recovered my ability to hear myself think and once again gained access to rivers of ideas and saw solutions to work problems, paths out of mazes that had once led me to dead ends. And as I reclaimed my creativity, I reclaimed my sense of self, my authentic identity.

Once reassembled as my true self, I could put aside the world of struggle. I no longer had to work against the current, against what was the wrong version of me. I crafted enterprises that connected with my ideal clients and achieved escape velocity because my market could now see and hear me. The real me. I no longer had to shout against the din of

"If you can get to
the root of who you are,
and make something
happen from it, my
sense is you're going to
surprise yourself."

Vidal Sassoon

competing voices. Living, working, and being from the core of my true self emanated a potent signal, landing on hearts and ears seeking precisely what I offered.

Little by little, I came to learn what inspiration actually means. That it is not an idea or solution to a problem delivered by generous gods of creativity in a sudden burst of illumination. Rather, inspiration comprises the vital "breathing in" acts of refueling and refilling the reservoirs of our soul, spirit, and stores of energy. That it is the "sourdough starter" of our creativity. Inspiration is the raw material for offers that connect and convert, for our competitive advantage, and for our market fit, all of which drive our business success.

Inspiration is what we are passionate about, what we find breathtaking and beautiful. It is blissful moments of being lost and in a state of flow while making something, working our hands, and letting our minds nap. Without inspiration—this joyful infusing and breathing into the center of us—we have nothing to offer that has the shape and stamp of our uniqueness.

When we are without inspiration, we are hollow husks, looking outward to what others are doing. We are tempted to follow suit, ignoring our own visions and voices. We may even measure our value (or lack thereof) against the apparent successes of the thundering other.

Without stores of inspiration, erasing our boundaries becomes first nature to us, and we routinely erode one of our most precious assets: our sacred, creative energy. We let others' agendas drive our own. We leap to our inboxes and phones. We honor interruptions, distractions, and habits that dull our trains of thought, our senses, and our shine.

Bringing myself alive did not happen all at once or in an instant. It was a series of experiences and lessons learned over the course of many years. In this book, I have taken each of these lessons and distilled them into the essential guidance I know to be of highest impact and leverage, saving you precious time and providing you with a path to accelerated, enduring results.

This book is a series of nautical charts to guide you to the islands of your heart's desires. To reclaim your power and put your true self back at the helm of your life. To open up to stunning inspiration and boundless play that connects you in profound ways to your creativity, intuition, and genius. This book will show you how to live and work with rapturous vibrancy and an ability to create your way to freedom each day. You'll learn how to be so attractive to the marketplace that you draw your ideal clients to you without the need for "push" marketing efforts. I'll show you how to arrive at the end of your life with no regrets, filled to the brim with having lived resonant, transformational experiences, expressed yourself creatively, shared countless moments with those you love most, and made your indelible mark upon the world so you leave it better than when you arrived.

While this book is geared toward entrepreneurs, many other creators, such as artists, students, educators, visionary leaders, and advocates of social change, will also benefit from the content.

The guidance I offer here is simple, though not necessarily easy. I understand all the reasons you want to close this book now and return it to the shelf. Your intuition, though, is to keep going. Please do. You and the world will be so glad you did.

I want to encourage each of your first attempts. The willingness to get it all wrong. The stepping into the new adventure with presence of mind and heart and the reserves to handle the uncertainty. With the release of this book, I, too, am pushing off from shore in a way I've never done. I can already feel the early signs of motion sickness as the horizon moves up and down, and the safety of the shore grows more distant.

We can do this together.

The day is sunny. The sky is clear. We have dry clothes and enough wind in our sails. Know there will be a time soon when none of these things is true. We will still reach our desired ports of call.

The essence of the voyage we are all on is the getting going—whether or not we feel prepared—and the staying going—whether or not we feel prepared. This work is not a one-and-done effort. It is work we do each day. Even though I am committed to suiting up to engage in creativity-feeding, inspirational practices every morning, I still have moments, most days, when I begin to negotiate with myself, bartering for the opportunity to slack off. I'll believe the lie that I can let my journaling, art practice, and meditating slide for a day or two without consequence. That I'm done filling the inspiration pipeline and can back off. *I'm proved wrong with harsh regularity that I cannot skip the inhale phase of creativity. Ever.*

While there's no graduation march, there is a light and joy-filled way we will learn to experience ourselves and the world, carried by the current of our creativity, bobbing up and down with impossible, delicious buoyancy.

Let's get to the balcony of our lives to see all the ways we are not free. All the ways we are numb, rudderless, and unable to feel our own hearts or know our own intuition. It's time to disentangle ourselves from those invisible perfectionist threads that are sending potent toxins into our bodies, minds, and souls. We will remember who we truly are, and we will create successful businesses and lives with purpose and ease from this powerful agency and alignment.

I'm reminded of a brilliant businesswoman, Claire (all clients' names have been changed), who came to me for help as she was transitioning out of a very successful yet soul-deadening enterprise into a new venture that had been calling to her heart for years. This once confident powerhouse did not trust her ability to do the work that brought her alive. The work that extinguished her signature spark and zapped her zeal—she could do that in her sleep, of which she got very little. No problem. Pain was familiar. Turning toward her own happiness, though, was foreign and frightening.

Claire hired me to take her on a coaching adventure back to her creative confidence so she could rediscover what fed her energy and how to fiercely protect it. Little by little, she remembered all the reasons the new enterprise called to her so strongly. She became unwilling to ignore her true self any longer.

She fought mightily against doing each exercise I presented to her, and again, I suspect this will be true for you as well. Our cultural training runs deep. We find it hard to believe that taking care of ourselves and dropping into our endless creativity are going to be the skeleton key for unlocking our happiness and improving our lives and businesses.

Eventually, Claire stopped pushing back and relented. She found early evidence that there was truth in my methodology and doubled down on doing the soul-stretching practices. Today, she is the proud and uber-successful owner of a business that represents her in every regard. Not the fabricated self or the facade she presented to the world for decades, but who she is at her core.

Claire's enterprise is now in its fifth year of operation, and she reports that her daily work feels like a giant sandbox of possibility and fun. She still texts me to celebrate evidence of her enduring transformation—moments when she has booked time away to reflect and rejuvenate, stopped on the side of the road to make a quick sketch to remember something that caught her eye, or registered another record-breaking quarter.

While the details vary, the storyline for all of my clients stays the same. We all share a similar "before" picture: stuck, weighty with armor, wandering in the woods of confusion, depleted and hiding out, with limited reach and influence. Our "after" picture is one of liberation, lightness of being, clarity, elevated energy, and visibility brought to life by vulnerability— with playful, unlimited impact.

Each time I begin working with a client, I make a promise: *I won't let you give up on yourself.* I make this promise to you now. Let's set sail.

Why I've Chosen Nautical Imagery and Metaphors for This Book

In the summer of 2020, I sat on the back deck of a cottage in my hometown of Highlands, North Carolina, looking up through towering oak and maple canopies to the sky. I watched the treetops sway and let myself become lightly hypnotized. I needed to choose a title for my book, and realized I wanted it to represent the state of being I wished for readers as they read the book, worked through the exercises, and folded what they learned into their businesses and daily lives. I wanted them, you, to feel the way the sea makes me feel.

For a child raised in the Appalachian Mountains, the sea represents a wild, limitless, unpredictable, mysterious energy. An expansive body that invites us to harness its vast power, pushing forward on waves as they transmit energy through the water. Through us.

For me, the sea and all nautical imagery are symbols of vacation, play, time with family, being unburdened by responsibility. During family trips to the Atlantic coast and Snug Harbor, to my grandparents' property in Key Largo, I could float, weightless, on salty swells. The sea gave me a sense of well-being, that everything was going to be just fine.

Childhood moments at the shore opened me to possibility and filled me with a willingness to surrender to adventure.

I want the metaphors in this book to help free us from our old fear-based thinking and behavior so we can stand, face tilted to the sun and breeze, graceful and confident inside our skin. So we can work in concert with the tides of who and what we love, harnessing the wind power of our optimal schedules to bring ease and flow to our work and creativity.

Buoyant.

In a buoyant state, we know and live who we truly are. Buoyant is how we feel when we work and live from our empowered and creative selves.

Inspired by mythologist Joseph Campbell's template of human transformation called "the hero's journey," I created a coaching methodology called the Creative Rebel's Voyage. This methodology maps the action steps of the changes I needed to embrace to breathe new life into my core, my enterprises. I took each insight and process I had experienced over twelve years and codified them into a recipe for my coaching clients to follow.

When we embark on and complete a Creative Rebel's Voyage, we feel buoyant. The Creative Rebel's Voyage stirs us up! Life-giving, nutrient-rich sediment that has settled onto the ocean floor of us becomes fully incorporated throughout our business and personal ecosystems, bringing us new energy, clarity, and courage. It teaches us how to release any addiction to emotions, thoughts, habits, and actions that do not serve us or our enterprises.

The Creative Rebel's Voyage is how we become wildly successful, creative, and free. I define success by much more than monetary abundance—although, of course, that is a key success metric. Success also comprises health, loving relationships, adventure and travel, inspired learning, personal and

Freedom + Success

Protect + Fuel Your Creative Energy

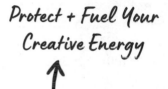
START HERE
Inspired Action

Put Your True Self at the Helm

Creating + Art Making

Self-Trust + Agency

professional growth, creative expression, doing work that matters and fosters positive change in the world, working from our strengths and delegating the rest, healthy habits and rituals, a peaceful mind and embodied calm, bold living and creating, and being unburdened from limiting beliefs. Freedom.

In other words, success is not just about hitting business metrics, dialing up cash flow, and fine-tuning the bottom line. It's not feeling slightly better while adhering to the notion that entrepreneurship must be a grind. It's about setting yourself truly free by taking an ordinary life and business, with all their flaws and limits, and making both extraordinary and remarkable. Completely in alignment with who we want to be and how we want to live and work.

By opening this book and reading its first pages, you have begun your own Creative Rebel's Voyage, your transformational journey. I invite you to embrace the ebbs and flows of this adventure, take the energy of the sea into your cells, and transfer its power into your marrow.

Breaking
Free

"Sail away from the
safe harbor. Catch the trade
winds in your sails.
Explore. Dream. Discover."

MARK TWAIN

HIS NUMBER popped up on my phone screen and my heart leapt out of rhythm. A jolt of excitement darted through my stomach, and I was alert with curiosity. How long had it been now? Nine years? I slid my legal pad over, picked up my favorite fountain pen, and tapped the green answer and speaker buttons in quick succession. After a few polite questions about how I was doing, Paul made his way to the reason for his call.

"Love your column in the newspaper," Paul said. "Been watching for it ever since your first one was published. Your approach to helping entrepreneurs reclaim their creativity is... uh... well, a revelation. In many respects, it's groundbreaking work for business owners, especially those of us who are on the edge of burnout."

"Thank you," I said. "That's very kind and generous of you to say." I could feel my pulse inside my ears as tingly rivers coursed up the back of my neck. I lowered my wrist to the pad. A thin ribbon of blue ink left the nib and lay on the surface in a tiny pool before soaking into the paper.

I blinked several times to process the power of the moment. Getting an unsolicited call from an entrepreneur like him was precisely what I had been working toward, dreaming of, for years. Even more amazing was to receive a call from him specifically, since he and his fellow board members were the very ones I was so desperate to win over during my Pitch-from-Hell moment in the summer of 2009.

I REMEMBER checking the mirror in the bathroom before I walked into the pitch meeting. Big mistake. Nothing fit anymore. My jacket was tight across my shoulders, and my blouse gaped open between two buttons at my sternum. I tried to tame my frizzy hair, but the humidity had already won. I wiped my sweaty palms on the sides of my skirt and took a deep breath. I really needed a yes today.

I turned the lever to the conference room door and walked in. Many more people than I had anticipated filled the tight space. Eyes met mine, and all the talking stopped. Paul, the board chairman, smiled and gestured toward an empty seat. After a brief introduction, the floor was mine. I rose and launched right into my presentation.

About two minutes in, I knew it was game over. One of the most important decision makers had her arms tightly folded against her chest, her lips pursed, her eyes narrowed—a textbook example of being closed off. The other major player kept his back to me while I spoke. I looked from his back to Paul, who seemed to be as confused as I was. The thimbleful of confidence I had come in with had evaporated, replaced by the uncomfortable knowledge that I was wasting their time. They feigned politeness and let me finish.

The next ten minutes or so are blocked from my memory, sealed off and vaulted to protect me from shame. I can vaguely recollect the heat in my face, which I worried was glowing red. I took a few questions, thanked everyone, and bolted.

I made it to my car before I started crying. I drove home and collapsed onto the sofa. Copies of my presentation along with my flip chart and markers lay in a chaotic heap at my feet. My head throbbed. I swallowed hard to keep down whatever was trying to bubble up from my boiling stomach.

Weeks of preparation, a killer idea: DOA. What had happened in that room? How come they couldn't see how my pitch was the solution to every challenge they had? And why had they treated me as if I were reading shocking and sensitive lab results aloud when, in fact, I was showing them a direct path to a goldmine of new revenue?

Back to square one. My fledgling consulting business was near the end of the runway, and the engines were quiet. No sign whatsoever of imminent liftoff. How was I going to get this bird airborne? I indulged in a few minutes of catastrophizing. I thought of the unopened bills on the corner of my desk and saw in my mind's eye the doomsday clock of impending foreclosure ticking down in hideous, neon-red digits.

I heard the faint whine of the school bus engine as it wound along the narrow gravel road toward our driveway. The kids would be home any minute. I had to pull myself together, stat.

"I HOPE you know I'm sincere," Paul said, jolting me out of my memories and bringing me back to the present. "It's clear you have been on some kind of transformational journey, right?"

When I didn't respond, he filled the silence.

"I'm deeply curious about what you've been up to and what you've discovered," he said. "It's evident you've stumbled onto something powerful. And whatever it is, it is profoundly contributing to your work with entrepreneurs. It's different from anything I've ever read about in business books. You're different. You seem so clear and confident now. Whatever you've been doing has filled you with a new vibrancy. It's inspiring. I'm wondering if you could help shepherd such change for my business ... and for me."

I doodled on the side of the pad while he spoke. I drew spirals and geometric shapes. Next to an entire series of exclamation points, I wrote the words "transformational journey." I was going back and forth in time, between the pitch meeting and the present. Fading in and out like a black-and-white movie clip. The contrast between the two scenes was sharp, powerful. I was now a magnet, sending out signals to those I wanted to serve. I had the attention of the market and had begun attracting business to me.

Paul and I set up a time to meet for breakfast at a local restaurant and explore ways I could work with his team and him. When we ended the call, I stared at the blue scribbles on the yellow paper until they blurred together. I bobbed up and down in a new, most welcome state of being. An elated state of confidence and clarity. I felt ... buoyant. I knew I could live and work in a joyful way that coaxed out of me the best of my creativity. My intuition that I could put down the white-knuckled struggle and instead exist outside the realm of anxiety had proved accurate. By embracing an inspired approach, I could harness the power of sailing with the tide in concert with the current of creativity within me, in flow.

I now had evidence my hunches were right. I definitely *was* onto something powerful. Ideal clients like Paul could now see the real me and recognize that I possessed novel, exciting solutions for escaping the entrepreneurial quagmire. I had the beginnings of a methodology that would illuminate the way out of failure and fear not only for me, but also for my clients.

WHEN MY business and personal life collapsed, I sent up a flare and looked for help. What I found were various versions of what I would come to understand was the status quo business advice to entrepreneurs who are stuck and riddled with self-doubt: acquire more discipline, develop new and better strategies, and execute on higher productivity by hustling harder.

This advice was perfectly seductive to me because it was a complete fit for what I believed to be true about myself and my abilities: I didn't have the right strategies or latest productivity hacks. I needed to buckle down, be more skilled in managing my enterprise. Even though I was working more than seventy hours a week, I believed I wasn't working hard enough. That *I* wasn't enough.

To be fair, I did find value in traditional business literature and coaching. It served as a tourniquet on my most urgent wounds and patched me up long enough to seek, find, and create more holistic, comprehensive, and enduring solutions. Solutions that would not only address the challenges in my business, but also rebuild me from the ground up and become the compass for a new way of achieving success as an entrepreneur.

I also saw that the standard counsel to entrepreneurs was incomplete and began searching for truth. For example, while one of the top reasons typically cited for why businesses fail is not having enough cash, I discovered that the underlying reasons for the cash crunch are often a lack of resourcefulness fueled by creative insight, as well as an inability to pull your market toward you.

Why is it that we cannot pull our market right toward us, and instead feel invisible to our ideal clients? Because we are invisible to ourselves. When we are energetically and creatively bankrupt, very little of what we say or do resonates or connects. All of our promotional efforts, slick sales copy, and banging of marketing gongs is distorted, muffled, and ignored, as none of it rings true with our intended audiences.

No creativity, no connection. No connection, no cash.

Being invisible to myself and my desired market was my initial challenge in finding traction and making sales. I was like the Headless Horseman, completely disconnected from my body and galloping through a life that bore no resemblance to who I truly was. I had always used my body as a transport mechanism for my head (as the late British education guru Sir Ken Robinson would say), living, working, and being from the cerebral part of me, overriding my heart with grotesque regularity. I trusted only my brain, my intelligence. My heart and body were routinely shushed, asked to be neither seen nor heard.

I craved time to think—to be able to hear the still voice emanating from within. The voice I knew had never lost hope. The voice of the five-year-old version of me, on her knees, begging me to wake up. But I drowned that out too. In my quest to stomp out feelings, the strategic and wise part of me got swept up in the undertow.

I'd stem the pain of the disconnect by numbing out with food, wine, nonstop work, and Olympic denial, all of which, of course, further fueled the distance between my head and heart. And in the process, I quashed all creative expression, even though I had dreamed of being a writer and an artist since childhood.

What I did have was throbbing anxiety, a tenor chord of feeling wildly out of control, and what felt like ancient sadness. Sadness that I had been carrying in my cells for decades.

I had also become proficient in perpetually scanning the environment for danger or doom. Something for my brain to "work on," to "fix." I had decided early on in my life that it was my job to hold up the world, solo. Be everyone's Atlas. Exhausting.

All of this squirrel-like scurrying around appeared on the surface to be working. Inside, though, I knew I was living on borrowed time. I could hear the roar of the falls ahead and sense the edge approaching as mist hit my face.

A sinking realization set in: I was at an inflection point. One choice would take me through straight-line winds of uncertainty toward the life and business I dreamed of. The other would take me further into more pain, suffering, and distance from my true destiny and joy. What had gotten me this far was not sustainable. The first burst of creativity I had when I launched my business, born out of my passion for building something new, had faded long ago because I had neglected every spring that could feed my blossoming, inspired creativity. I had hit what I now call the dreaded Stagnation Zone.

The Stagnation Zone is my term for the painful quagmire of lackluster sales and anemic traction in the market. When we get bogged down in it, color drains from our personal lives and businesses, and we enter a fog of anxiety and exhaustion, amplified by a loss of connection to our inherent power. We know we are in the Stagnation Zone when nothing we do or say seems to resonate or land with our ideal clients.

Once I realized I was in this quagmire, I began thrashing to free myself. I first reached for the branch of doubling down on higher levels of self-sacrifice, believing the cure-all would be unlocked with a strategy involving caffeinating, bucking up, and fighting with aggressive, unending action. This surge of action was simply more of the same and just increased my exhaustion, anxiety, and doubt. My bucket of sacred energy was pierced with holes and leaking everywhere as I denied myself happiness, rest, and play as well as connection to beauty, art, and nature. I eventually stopped reaching for branches to pull myself out of the churning foam of doing and surrendered to what was now my daily reality. I drifted, like an unmoored boat, further and further away from the pier of my authentic self and my creativity.

Shame descended upon my shoulders. I had always prided myself on my perfectionism and over-achievement. Success in my enterprise gave me the validation and sense of worth I desperately sought, but those balloons of self-confidence were now pierced, zigzagging over my head as they deflated.

I now doubted everything, from my entrepreneurial acumen to the original concept for my business to how I had structured my company's daily operations. I let the decline in my health accumulate and disassociated from my body.

As I dug oar after oar into the water trying to turn the boat around, a friend offered me sweet comfort and permission to stop all the striving. "When something breaks," she said, "the energy contained within it needs to be released, so that something new can be born in its place."

This insight pierced me to the core. I had had enough of the pain, overwhelm, and grief and began to embrace the idea of simply allowing my old ways of being and working to break. And break me open in the process. I was done with the bad taste in my mouth over not being my true self and wearing the heavy suit of barrier flesh. I was ready to unzip and step out and away from all of the anchors.

I chose to break free and thus embarked on an extensive journey. I started with only a sputtering pilot light of willingness. It was enough. And it will be enough for you too.

During my Pitch-from-Hell moment, I had been out of sync with my voice and rhythm because I lacked confidence and wasn't seated in powerful, resonant energy and messaging. I didn't trust what I had to offer and I gave off mixed signals: on the one hand, elements of the solutions I proposed were intriguing; on the other, there was a disconnect that made the people in the room doubt that I was the right person to lead the charge. They intuited that something was *off.*

Once I began recovering my creativity by changing my daily habits and rituals, things shifted. My sense of self warmed and shone. I became devoted to infusing my spirit with what lifted my gaze toward possibility and craft. I learned how to tolerate uncertainty, see in the dark, and hear what wasn't being said, as I cultivated deep levels of empathy. I became astute in paying attention and picking up signals from the market, overt and tacit. My business and my body took on entirely new and healthy shapes.

I thought of the parable of the Golden Buddha as told in the captivating film *Finding Joe.* There was a huge statue of the Golden Buddha in a Thai village. The villagers received news that an army from a neighboring country was going to invade their monastery. To hide and protect the Buddha from being looted, they covered it in mud and concrete. Their plan worked. Years passed and no one remembered the Golden Buddha, until a young monk noticed a piece of concrete had broken off and saw the shiny gold underneath. He alerted his fellow monks, and they worked together to free the Buddha from its prison.

The metaphor in this parable is that we are all born golden, connected to our truth, to divinity. Over time, our parents, teachers, culture, and peers pass on messages upon messages about how to behave, think, and feel. As we fold those messages into our hearts and minds, we develop multiple layers of concrete that mask and then hide our authentic selves. Then something happens that knocks off a piece of our protective casing. It could be a devastating or tragic event like financial strife, a health crisis, the loss of a loved one, or a divorce. Or it could be a jubilant moment of personal transformation, new awareness, or a turning point that leads our path toward greater happiness and knowledge.

Once our true nature is revealed, even if only one square inch of our gold, we now have a taste of the ease of alignment. We endeavor to blast away the remaining layers that hide us, keep us stuck. We mindfully sculpt away the chunks of cement that have accumulated on us, the hardened gray matter composed of the expectations of others and oxygen-thinning limiting beliefs. Layer by layer, we loosen the confining casing that has weighed us down into hunched and distorted figures. We can choose to set out upon a Creative Rebel's Voyage and leave the shores of comfort and perceived safety, let ourselves be tested, and return having been changed in great and small ways.

I wondered what else was possible. How far could I take this new way of thinking and being? How much more concrete could I chisel away to reveal the entire gold me? And how could I leverage that knowledge and help others blast away their own strata of encasing, hardened muck?

This book contains each lesson I learned, each line on the nautical chart. Every transformational morsel. Throughout, I will challenge the advice you have most likely been given over and over during your years as an entrepreneur. This routine advice is not entirely wrong—it just does not offer us a complete or humane map. We are conditioned to believe that creativity is trivial, inconsequential. Something to do when we are bored or have time to kill.

Instead, creativity is the missing link in our business success and personal fulfillment. We must bring it forward and place it first. We must incorporate it into our daily lives if we are going to empower ourselves and attract what has always felt just out of reach.

When we narrow our focus, inhabiting a world of anxious striving in a futile attempt to efface some intrinsic sense that we're not good enough, we cut off the oxygen supply to our buoyant, creative selves. Our charge, then, is to open the petals of our true selves, one by one, joyfully conscious that when we focus on inspiring the art of us, on the very things that make us insanely attractive to our ideal clients, we bring the success we seek right to us.

Paradoxically, most of us are absolutely crystal clear on what it is we do *not* want. The details of the lives we find abhorrent and crazy-making are cemented in our minds. Having that intel is a good start. But too many of us stop there. We think we will find a life of freedom by avoiding only the feelings we do not want to feel, the people we do not want to engage with, and the tasks that dull us and fill us with dread.

We are gifted in our numbing choices, artful. We survive inside small, rubber life rafts we fashion out of overwork, consumption of media, and emotional and physical fatigue. We strive to quench internal flames with alcohol, stuff down feelings with food, and zone out, hunched over our phones.

We forget that we already have a ticket out of hell in our coat pocket—that is, figuring out what and whom we love, what fills us with pleasure and joy. We forget to focus on creating and enjoying the small, daily moments that connect us to what resonates with us, what satiates and stimulates our curiosity, and straightens the spine of our soul as if to whisper or shout, "Yes!"

My message to entrepreneurs and creators who are painfully stuck and riddled with self-doubt is simple: We can heal our businesses and our lives. Our enterprises and our moment-to-moment enjoyment of life are inexorably interconnected; practices, habits, and rituals that benefit one, benefit the other. We begin by understanding that the success strategies we've been taught are, at best, incomplete.

It's time for a renaissance in how we approach entrepreneurship and living an artful life. I will offer a new way back to your agile, joyful self while revealing how to discover an easier path to success and freedom by tapping into the power of unbridled access to inspiration.

How to Get the Most Out of This Book and Approach the Exercises

Let's adopt a playful approach to reading this book and doing the exercises. There is no one right way to do either, and I encourage you to lean into what feels right for you.

You may consider the following options:

- Read the entire book through, beginning to end, stopping to do each exercise.

- Read and do the associated exercises in no particular order, dipping in and out.

- Read the book all the way through without doing the exercises, and then reread it and do each of the exercises on the second pass.

You will note the exercises are placed at the end of certain sections and chapters and are marked with an icon of a journal and pen. This is your signal to pause your voyage, tie off, and do some work. Some exercises are followed by sections called Inspiration Beacons. These are prompts offering opportunities for further reflection, expanded thinking, and idea generation.

I suggest approaching the exercises with a "25/5" structure. That is, commit to spending a minimum of twenty-five minutes a day, five days a week doing the exercises. You may opt for a Monday to Friday schedule, or perhaps a Monday, Wednesday, Friday, Saturday, Sunday routine fits your life better. Note that shorter and more frequent work sessions are much more effective than longer, less frequent ones. Frequency keeps us connected to our inspiration and willingness and helps defang our fear and bolster our courage for tolerating the unknown.

If you can do only five minutes a day, start there. There were many days when that was all I could muster. The power of showing up, even briefly, accumulates and still yields benefits, bestowing upon us little nuggets of restored senses of self.

In addition to establishing a routine, it is important to understand some basic tenets of human behavior at the outset so that you can stay aware throughout.

Know that within us is a muscle memory urging us to race like stallions toward the promises of productivity, and that we will have to consciously work this notion out of our bodies and impulses. Know that we may scoff at and resist doing the exercises in this book.

Understand not only that our resistance is born of a belief that play, creativity, and inspiration are frivolous and child-like, but also that as we engage in practices that scooch us up to what we are truly feeling, we will panic a little and want to turn and run.

Every time I want to get up and quit one of these practices, or avoid doing this work altogether, I sit back down and ask myself: What is it that I do not want to think or feel right now? I quickly write down whatever comes up. Over the course of more than a decade, I have found that my answers and my clients' answers generally fall into the following categories:

- I don't want to feel I am wasting my time. (I have so much other work to do right now.)

- I don't want to feel the pain of xyz memory, thought, or belief.

- I don't want to feel the uncertainty of doing this practice.

- I don't want to think that what I make isn't any good.

- I don't want to feel the ick of incompetency, of not being good at certain tasks.

- I don't want to feel the vulnerability and exposure of doing this work.

- I don't want to feel the judgment from myself or others as I do this work.

Your answers will most likely look very similar.

Be warned: If we let ourselves remain unconscious and let avoidance behavior go unaddressed, *nothing will change for us.*

Fortune favors the brave. And if you are not brave yet, that's okay. You just need to be willing to stop trying to *think* your way through and start *creating* your way through. The more we create, the more powerful we become.

Know that we are not unlike wild animals who need continual soothing, compassion, reassurance, and settling down. We need to keep coaxing our wary and untrusting selves back to the table, back to the practices, back to the daily work.

Easy does it.

The Alchemical Power of Journaling

No one wants to be under the piercing glare of judgment. The mere thought of it can make us cringe, and our fear of it can keep us small, invisible, hiding from vulnerability. The desire to avoid harsh judgment pushes us to strive to live and work in a place where there are no errors, no failures of any size or scope, no attempts that fizzle or fall flat.

As a result, we can exist in a "push me, pull you" relationship with our own creativity. The ideas come, and for a moment or two we'll begin to flesh them out in our minds. We'll start to explore their potential and maybe even take a step or two in action. Then the curtain of fear of judgment

"To keep a journal is to learn how to play. Deeply."

Alexandra Johnson

falls. And back we go into the stage wings. Into darkness, out of view. Out of action and out of the zone of possibility.

This anxiety weighs us down and locks us into place. If we routinely stop listening to and/or acting on our own ideas, we stop generating them. Frozen in place, we'll look to distraction, numbing out, or overdoing to release the pressure building within us. Creativity is like a rushing current. It wants to move. Dammed up, it becomes a toxic pond with swirls of algae blooms on its stagnant surface.

Our stalwart defense against paralyzing inertia? A journal. Seemingly powerless and small next to our fear, a journal can transport us to the shores of safety and calm. By writing, sketching, painting, or collaging in our journals, we can turn the valve and release the river of our creativity.

A journal is where we work things out. Where we air our frustrations, worry, anger, pain. A place where we celebrate, exalt, express our joy. It is a protected zone where we can take risks, try on ideas, and search for connections and solutions. A journal is our atlas to the world of possibility. When we have a lock on a state of possibility, we find opportunities everywhere.

Our journal can be a luxurious, leather-bound volume, a traveler's notebook, a sketchbook, or a spiral-bound notebook with yellowed pages and curling corners, purchased from a discount store. It can be loose sheets of paper, gathered from here and there, kept inside a folder. Our journal is whatever we want it be, in whatever form we prefer. The key is that we use it, that we show up and do the work.

In our journal, we work through our reluctance. We find our way out of being stuck, hacking through mental weeds. Once we finally begin to let go, we revel in the freedom a journal affords us. We can return to our natural state of being playful, willing to not know.

I know the excitement and promise of a brand-new journal. It's pristine, unmarred. There are no traces of past errors.

According to us, our journal is somehow better when it is new and its pages do not contain mistakes, reflections of what we consider were bad choices. A theme with which we are rather familiar in other areas of our lives and business.

Your journal will be one of many thresholds on your voyage. On one side is the world of the closed, unused book, the painful clinging to perfection that has kept you stuck, unwilling to try new ideas, explore. On the other is an opened book, pages filled, and the world of possibility and play.

Your journal is your place to try on new ideas, take risks, make mistakes, think things through, navigate uncertainty, record insights and intuition, sketch to see, paste images of things that bring you joy, and purge your brain of tumbling thoughts that drain your focus and energy. Your journal is your portal of discovery.

You will find that as you fill the pages of your journal, you'll delight in its odd, irregular, imperfect vibrancy, and how it reflects the energy of who you are. You will no longer want to keep it closed and new; instead, you will seek ways to amp up its patina and signs of wear. You will recognize yourself in the pages, remember what brings you alive, and be exhilarated by creating pages filled with ink, graphite, and scraps of this and that. As you leaf through it, your journal's sometimes chaotic pages will remind you to take it easier on yourself, to let yourself off the hook, to delight in your fieldwork of becoming.

Your journal is your partner, the logbook of your voyage. You will return to it again and again, not just while you are reading this book, but throughout your life. The work you do in its pages will guide you no matter where you choose to set sail. Use it, mark it up, mess it up, fill it up. The more of you that you pour onto its pages, the brighter of a beacon it will be for you. And when you reach the last page, store it in a visible place so that you will be prompted to return to it time and again to mine it for ideas. Then, crack open a new one. Keep the momentum going.

"We must cultivate our own garden," French philosopher and author Voltaire advocated in his novella *Candide*. My interpretation of his ethos is that we all must discover what it is that drives us, excites us, and fills us with passion and joy. What is it that we think, value, and hold dear? Whom and what do we love? Until we know these basic things about ourselves, we cannot venture toward bringing more of them into our daily experience and enjoyment of life. Knowing what these elements are for us allows us to orient our focus toward the ports of call we want to inhabit fully.

To achieve these breakthroughs, we must first break through to what lies within the seed of us.

Now, let's gently lower ourselves into the water with a short exercise. Crack the spine of your journal, whether it be sparkling new or well worn, and prepare to lay down some graphite or ink on a pristine page.

exercise What Do You Love? And What Are Your Anchors?

Turn your journal sideways, and in the center of the page, write the following in big letters: *What is it I love? What is it I live for?*

Now, without overthinking it, begin writing your answers all around those two questions. You might choose to think about some of the happiest times in your life. What were you doing? With whom? Where were you? Or you may consider your answers from the perspective of what it is you value, then list them accordingly. Work quickly so that you can override any self-judgment or censoring. Fill the page.

Congratulations! You now have banked your first wins. You have not only broken in your journal and thinking, but also crossed through the first of what will be many liberating gateways. What lies on the journal page in front of you is essential, foundational self-knowledge.

Next, can you readily identify and rattle off the anchors in your life and business? What, specifically, is holding you underwater? I would imagine those things occupy quite a bit of your daily bandwidth and focus. Ongoing issues that you vow to someday remedy, but that you simply haven't known how to tackle. Don't worry about the "hows" right now; we will address how to loosen them as we move through the book. Take a few moments and list your anchors in your journal. Capture them all in their hideous, steely character and notice how the simple act of getting them all down brings relief.

Inspired Creating Is the Surprising Answer You Seek

You may feel defensive after reading this section's title, ready to make it clear to everyone that you are not an artist, not creative. Besides, how is that even relevant? Can't we just get on with the advice on how to heal your personal life and find business traction and success?

I get it. I used to feel the same way. What I'm about to share goes against everything we tend to believe, how we measure our worth, and how we calibrate our actions to justify our ability to take up space and oxygen. At the core of it is a practice that is done for the experience and *not* the results. It is the very opposite of how our minds and souls are trained.

"Creating art is about growing the world and increasing its reach, and it has more to do with the act of creation itself than what is actually made."

Nick Cave

Please suspend judgment for just a bit. The payoff and all-encompassing liberation will be completely worth it. Promise.

Let's begin with the feeling state that lies beneath most of our goals, wishes, and dreams: freedom. If we were to reverse-engineer the goals of financial success (freedom to spend our time as we choose), optimal health (freedom of movement, lightness of being, confident centeredness), plentiful adventure and play (freedom of exploration and discovery), giving and receiving unconditional love (freedom of expression and freely connecting with others while truly being seen and heard), and/or uplifting work and transformational experiences (freedom to do the work we find most meaningful and freedom to impact the world), the bread crumb trail would lead us straight back to our desire for freedom.

And underneath our desired state of freedom lies one central concept: agency. *Merriam-Webster* defines agency as "the capacity, condition, or state of acting or of exerting power." Now, let's be clear: I am talking about reclaiming your power. Power over the self, not over other people. Power to craft one's destiny. Power to create, moment to moment, how you want to feel. Power to choose. Power to align your soul with meaning. Power to bring your true self forward. Power to experience the ecstasy of being fully present and aware. Power to positively influence and impact yourself and others. Owning and reclaiming your power for good.

And guess what lies underneath achieving agency? Making art. Any art, any medium. Good, bad, recognizable, unrecognizable, fancy, plain. We can choose to head to the kitchen, the dance floor, the canvas, the blank sheet of paper, or the typewriter. We can pick up a chef's knife, a pair of dancing shoes, a brush, a pencil, or a pan of paint. The medium doesn't matter. Your skill level doesn't matter. The art form is irrelevant. You choose whatever calls to you. Whatever sounds fun. The act of getting going and making art is the only thing that matters. And guess what forms the raw material for making art?

Inspiration. Although most likely not in the way you think. Bestselling author Paulo Coelho has a gorgeous way of explaining what inspiration is and the power it holds over our destinies:

> What is inspiration? Inspiration is breathing in, right? So you put what is outside, inside of you, and then you expire [breathe out] ... It is connected with this energy that we don't understand ... it is connected with the energy of love ... Inspiration is a boat, and you are in this boat in a sea. So there is this gigantic sea, and your boat is taking you. Inspiration is guiding you. Inspiration is the wind that is guiding you towards your destiny. If you try to guide inspiration, you're lost.

My interpretation of Coelho's quote is that if we do not fill the lungs of our being with passion, beauty, art, love, and sumptuous experiences, we won't have the ability to breathe out creative acts. Just as it is true within the physical body, it is true within the body of the self. We must inspire first. Fill the wells within us. Fill the lungs of our being with fresh oxygen. There can be no breathing out, no creating, without it.

What we are trained to do, though, is deplete all of our creative resources, day in and day out, by yoking ourselves to a plow of discipline and more work. Lots and lots of exhaling. A relentless expenditure of energy that drains our tank and steals our creativity kindling. We are taught to consider the inspirational acts of play, creative expression, and immersing ourselves in wonder to be frivolous, childish, or for folks who are "crafty." We consider ourselves serious, business-minded adults, not children or leisurely folks with time to kill.

I know how surprising and unbelievable it is for me to say that making things, immersing ourselves in beauty, and intentionally curating our minds are just a few of the unexpected ways to get out of enterprise doldrums and the stress of repeatedly missing financial targets. After all, we understand and value work. Lots and lots of work. Play? Not so much.

Creativity isn't just a physical by-product of our artistic effort. Creativity is a swirling force of potentiality in our minds and spirits. It is infused in how we approach our engagement with and delight in living and working each day. It is both the fuel and the fire of our inspiration. It is also the vessel that carries us to who we truly are. It is a nautical chart that helps us map the ports of call that pull us, excite us, lift us, and bring light into the darkest places of our hearts and minds.

Inspiration and creativity work as playful co-conspirators of joy. They are both the point of departure and the moment of arrival, initiating and delivering us to a new point of departure.

The Rhythm of Access to Creativity

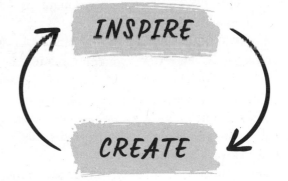

It wasn't until I first stepped onto the boat of inspiration that I came to understand firsthand that my all-work, no-play approach to entrepreneurship was not only minimizing my success but also stopping me from accessing insight during crucial moments. Once aboard, though, I became more acclimated to the experience of not knowing and letting myself feel the odd and scary space of uncertainty. Let time drop away, I told myself. Stop the rush of doing. Reinhabit your body and feel the stillness and the emotions that pop up like bubbles in a glass of soda. I began to not only let my intuition come to the fore, but also to trust it. How did I board the inspiration boat for the first time? Peaches.

Boarding the Boat of Inspiration: Sketching to See

It had been a typical day—I was on the phone nonstop, negotiating deals and working with real estate clients. By the time I arrived at The Bascom art campus, I felt as if my brain was pierced with dozens of sentence fragments, broken off and sharp from the day's conversations. I walked inside the building and inhaled the art that filled the main floor gallery. When I saw the grinning face of my art teacher, Knight, the crush of the day lifted immediately.

We ducked into a studio space and settled in. Knight had placed three peaches on a wooden table under a spotlight emanating from a lamp clipped to the side. "Sketch the peaches," he said, "taking special note of the shadows, curves, and contours." I nonchalantly sharpened a pencil with a few rotations and studied the peaches with a casual eye, trying to decide how to approach the sketch.

I wasn't sure how to begin or where to focus, so I leaned back in my chair, let my shoulders drop, and exhaled. I stopped seeking a strategy, which was my go-to, daily approach to living and working. I simply sat and really took in each peach. My eyes took me by the hand and led me into a place of beauty and awareness I had rarely experienced.

I began to cry.

I had seen peaches hundreds, maybe thousands of times before. But this was the first time I had actually *seen* peaches. I was captivated by every stunning detail, the miracle of these creations sitting in front of me. How perfectly each crevice, curve, and shadow revealed itself. Their astonishing colors, texture, and shape. I appreciated the divine design of each.

I also became deeply aware of what I had been missing my entire life. Yes, I had witnessed and appreciated beautiful things in nature, in the sweet faces of friends and loved ones, in galleries, on city streets, and in mountain towns and landscapes. But how often had I had blinders on during the course of each day, just roaring through the world without taking in the beauty around me? As the tears tracked down my cheeks, I realized with regret just how often that had been the case.

For the next two hours, I floated in an entirely new world, relearning how to see. My paper was thin and smudged from repeated erasing. Starts and stops. New attempts. I vacillated between feeling nauseated by overwhelming uncertainty and relieved when I stopped trying to control the outcome of my sketch. Curve by curve, graphite line by graphite line, an image appeared. I let go of the rope of perfectionism and felt the hemp fibers slide through my palms.

When the lesson was over, I had a sketch, my first intentional voyage in the boat of inspiration. And while I was pleased that the pencil lines on my sketchpad formed recognizable shapes, I knew I had so much more than a first drawing.

As I strained to teach my hands how to recreate an image, I began training my eyes and brain to see in new ways. With each stumble, each search for how to make the drawing, I discovered how to keep going, how to stay in an unresolved space with open loops of not knowing. I learned how unsafe and threatened I felt in uncertainty. I recognized how much I wanted the illusion of safety that comes from believing I know something for certain in both my business and life. As someone bent on tidying up and making problems go away, I watched my comfort zone disappear behind the horizon. I learned how to let myself get it wrong, to feel the piercing and raw and wildly uncomfortable waves. My time sketching helped me stretch out more comfortably on the rolling tides of doubt. This growing tolerance for unpredictability became a superpower. I left my lesson a different person.

I drove to the school bus stop and picked up my son, Adam. Once home, I placed all my art supplies on the kitchen counter and began surveying the refrigerator for dinner ideas. The phone rang, and I saw a client's name on the screen. I answered promptly.

My seller client skipped "Hello" and dove right into a rant. He had just opened his email to see his home inspection report and the request for a credit from the buyer. I tried to explain that we had lots of options as to how to respond, but he drove right past my comments and declared his ultimatum: the buyer's agent and I were to split the cost of the repairs. Period. That or the deal was off.

I didn't react. I didn't rush in to fix the problem while the tire tracks were still fresh on my forehead. I just paused, as I had done a couple of hours earlier when beginning my sketch. My client, who was accustomed to my jumping immediately each time he made a demand, was startled and confused.

He repeated, "Just so you understand, I'm not paying for this. *You* are!"

I shifted my shoulders to the left and let his shouting whiz by. Even though I had a grand total of $440 in my checking account, all I said was, "I'll communicate that to the buyer's agent."

He paused for a few seconds and said, "I expect you'll let me know immediately that you agree to handle this."

I emailed the buyer's agent and conveyed the seller's position. I then did something I had never done in more than a decade as a real estate professional, much less in the midst of a negotiation. I turned off my phone.

I made dinner and helped Adam with his homework.

At around nine that evening, Adam looked at my phone's dark screen and asked, "Aren't you going to call that man back?"

Adam wasn't really interested in whether or not I would call the seller. He was wondering if something was wrong with me. Had aliens abducted his mother and replaced her with a calm, detached lookalike?

I slid the phone over and turned it back on. The screen illuminated with notifications of missed calls, texts, and voicemails. I assumed the deal was dead. As I read and played back messages, it was clear the deal was very much alive. My client had panicked when I didn't immediately agree to pay for all the repairs with the other agent. The crush of uncertainty had been too much for him, so he had solved the problem himself by agreeing to pay for the repairs. We closed three weeks later, and I had a year's worth of burn rate in my checking account.

The boat of inspiration had taken me to new shores: a powerful place of agency. In the short period of time I spent sketching, I had begun to discover the outline of a new me and now had reassembling instructions. Instructions that reminded me that when I tilt my head back and let the light hit my face while opening up to and owning not knowing, my lungs expand, my brain settles, my shoulders drop, and my heart pumps without rushing the beat. Conversely, when I clamor for certainty, I close myself off from the world of unlimited possibilities, curiosity, and serendipity.

And finally, I discovered a hidden danger: If we cannot trust ourselves in times of uncertainty, we can fall prey to external pressures from others. We can lose our internal guidance system and strong stance of knowing and advocating for what it is we want to happen. We can cave to outside influences and demands that push us further away from who we truly are and the success and freedom we seek.

My first message in a bottle, plucked out of the sea and brought on board.

Once we make the shift to putting ourselves back at the helm of our own lives, we become powerfully intentional about every aspect of our work and life, beginning with ensuring that we infuse our souls with the elements that fuel us and our creativity, foster agency, and deliver freedom. And it is from there that we douse burnout and cultivate sustained impact and joy, witnessing the power of presence rippling throughout our businesses.

Are you more willing now to believe that you will not achieve the success and freedom you seek by doing more work, working smarter, or finding the latest magical strategy to really dial in your business and management acumen?

Are you a bit more open to accepting that success and freedom come from filling each cell of your awareness and daily life with inspiration in its myriad, delicious forms, opening you to your unbounded, creative heart?

Doing this work transformed me from being stuck in drudgery and dread to being freed to live and work in a new zone of fun and excitement. It led me from insecure waffling to decisive, confident action; from being exhausted with an empty tank to fired up on endless, renewable reserves of energy; from staying crouched and hidden to being vulnerable and open; and from untapped, stifled creativity to flowing, inspired expression. The people I most wanted to

serve could not only see and hear me, but they could also readily trust me because everything about who I was as a person
and how I behaved was aligned and coherent. Once I understood the power of inspiration, I could stop struggling and
inhabit the power of what makes me unique.

Happily, our ability to tap into inspiration is much closer
to us and easier than we think. Making art helps us return to
artful living in the present moment.

exercise Sketching

Give me eighteen minutes, tops. Set a timer.

Find an item to draw. It could be this book, your car key, or
a vase. Any item will work.

Note that there is only one rule of drawing: to see.

If you truly want to see something and experience it fully,
sketch it. Drop the notion that you do not know how to sketch.
You do know how. Simply get a piece of paper and a pencil and
begin. Follow the item's outside edge, its contour, with your
eye and let your pencil follow on the page. Send your inner
critic out on an errand to keep it busy and just relax into the
paper, your pencil, and the item you are drawing. The end
result on the page is not the point. The *experience* you have
while sketching is the point, as are your deepening awareness
and truly seeing.

As you drop into a state of greater presence, you will experience something that will initially feel a bit unfamiliar. It is the
feeling of moving into and working from the part of your brain
that is linked to your creative expression. When you leave the
linear world that focuses on language, logic, and order and

pass through the gates to imagination, holistic thinking, and intuition, you may shudder a bit as electricity courses through you. This marks the moment you begin shifting on an energetic, cellular level, as you gently open up to the world.

You may find you begin to document things you want to remember by capturing them with quick sketches. All the better! Give the camera on your phone a rest and pop out your journal and pencil instead. Sketch to see.

If you are hesitant to give this exercise a try, perhaps an old art-shaming incident is flashing back and haunting you. I've got plenty, and I know how those memories hold us back from trying to sketch, paint, or create anything. We reason that if we failed once at this art thing, we will certainly do so again. This is not a pass or fail exercise, however. Creating a sketch you are proud of is not the point (although you may do just that). In fact, try to make a truly awful sketch!

Ready? Set your timer for eighteen minutes. Here we go!

Opening Up to Inspiration

"I learned...that inspiration does not come like a bolt, nor is it kinetic, energetic striving, but it comes into us slowly and quietly and all the time."

BRENDA UELAND

WAS SIX YEARS OLD and happily lost in creative flow. It was a rainy summer day, and I sat at a long table in the Highlands Nature Center, coloring a rainbow trout I had drawn. I was delighted with my creation and worked with focus, ensuring each purple, yellow, red, green, and silver crayon brought life to each scale.

The tall girl from Florida, who was visiting the mountains for the summer, bumped the back of my chair as she walked behind me. She leaned over my right shoulder, peering down at my paper. Her long, straight hair fell forward and hung over my fish like a curtain. I was so proud of my picture that I shifted my shoulders to the left so she could get a better view.

"What *is* that?" she asked loudly.

Everyone at the table stopped working and looked up.

"I mean, what *isss* that?" she hissed, louder.

"A rainbow trout," I said quietly, staring down at my fish.

I knew I was under attack. A torrent of flight chemicals pushed through my veins, firehose-style. I didn't dare look up. I felt sick, embarrassed, and sad all at once.

"It's *ri-dic-u-lous*! No fish I know looks like *that*!"

A sweet boy across from me tried to throw me a life preserver. "Sure they do! Rainbows are full of color. I catch 'em all the time."

"Still ridiculous," she said with a huff. She jerked her raincoat from the hook on the wall and walked out the front door, where a car was waiting.

Dad was late picking me up, and I had time to replay the incident over and over in my mind. When his green Jeep pulled into the circular gravel driveway, I was almost in tears.

"Hi there, Charlie Banana!" he said, smiling as I got in. "Oh, let's see what you made!"

"It's just a silly fish . . ."

"Wow! Would you look at that! I think your use of color is spot on. Great detail. Your work shows so much thoughtfulness." He edged the Jeep toward Horse Cove Road. While looking for traffic over his left shoulder, he said, "Feel proud of your work. It is unique and beautiful."

I looked at my paper on the way home and decided it wasn't so bad, after all. Still, the tall girl from Florida had managed to set a small hook into my creative confidence, leaving behind a scar.

Every now and then, voices like hers—others who have criticized a drawing, a story, an essay, or anything else I have ever made—replace the sane, kind voices inside my head and pulverize my poise. They gather in a circle, around a campfire of meanness, and chant a chorus of insults that snuff out my willingness to try again.

Bestselling author and researcher Brené Brown says that you, too, have most likely been art-shamed:

> When I started the research on shame, you know, thirteen years ago, I found that 85 percent of the men and women who I interviewed remembered an event in school that was so shameful, it changed how they thought of themselves for the rest of their lives. But wait—this is good—50 percent of that 85 percent, half of those people: those shame wounds

were around creativity. So 50 percent of those people have art scars. Have creativity scars.

This is a common phenomenon. We are all in good company. What are *your* creativity scars?

exercise Healing Your Creativity Scars

Let's go back in time and bring up one of your most prickly, painful, art-shaming memories. Go back to the incident and bring it to mind clearly. Write it all down in your journal. Who was there? What happened? What did you feel? What did you think about your ability to create as a result? Capture all the nastiness in its full, gruesome glory.

Now, let's jump into a time machine together and rewrite history. Let's write and draw over your creative blocks.

Study the details of your art-shaming story and craft yourself a brand-new present and future. Decide what you want to *think and feel* now, all these years later. Next, decide what kind of images would best represent how you want to think and feel. For example, let's say you wanted to feel more courageous. You might choose to draw a stick figure in Superman's pose. Or, if you want to feel proud of your creative work, you might sketch out a big star. Joyful? Make a drawing of a big grin. Get down as many images of your newly desired state as you can.

Again, before you wince and say that you cannot draw, please know that what we are looking for here is a simple representation of your desired future and how you want to feel there. We aren't focusing on the quality of your sketch, although you may find it beautiful. Focus instead on drawing images that reflect how you want to feel when immersed in making something. Maybe your sketch will have illustrations that symbolize strength, confidence, happiness, freedom, flow, pride, accomplishment, ease, community, fire, or connection. Remember: Stick figures work well here! Or, if you prefer, write out the words in your journal that describe how you want to feel and add a tiny, illustrative flourish that brings each word to life for you.

Next, write the new vision as a reenactment of the art-shaming incident. Go back to the past as the wise and strong adult you are today and do things differently. Say things differently. Choose a different outcome.

Go crazy here if you want. You can choose to turn the painful memory into satire. Or you can create a completely outrageous series of events, with you as the hero or heroine of the story. You can talk back to the bullies with eloquence and piercing humor, leaving the onlookers stunned by your courage and cleverness.

Transmute your art-shaming trauma into a new energy.

We are each the writer, producer, and director of our life's story. And we are the artist who can sketch out our desired futures and bring those images into our reality.

We can step into our time machine at any hour and fashion a narrative that heals, lifts, and emboldens us to return to our power. We can topple and trounce our roadblocks and transform our scars into bridges that take us safely across the river of our history, sudsy with old shame. We can show up for ourselves, our work, and our clients and tame the inner and outer trolls whose opinions are none of our concern.

You may be a bit perturbed by the instructions to replay old memories that sting. You may also be apprehensive about trying to sketch, especially after reliving memories that have turned over the protective soil of you and exposed you to the bright sun of vulnerability. Please rally your courage and give it a go. It is essential work to do before we proceed to what comes next on our voyage: Learning how to open up to inspiration.

Do you remember the parable about the Golden Buddha in chapter 1? Do you recall his concrete exterior? Along with other suffering, the concrete encasing us is composed of each art-shaming incident we have endured. It could be one whopper of a moment or several smaller ones. Regardless, that concrete is real and it is keeping us from breaking through so we can sound our unique voices and try our tender hands again. So we can step into the spotlight and hold up our work. So we can show the thing we made that only we can make.

Unless we connect our chisel with the concrete by doing this healing work, we cannot open up to the sweet, rejuvenating power of inspiration. Without this work, we might graze against inspiration's vast vigor only to find that its medicine cannot penetrate our tough exteriors. Our soul's dermis will hold it at bay where its energy will be washed away like stormwater finding the lowest slope off a mountainside.

Go to your journal. Be curious. I promise you'll have at least one insight that will begin to unfold you, if even in the tiniest way.

Curating a Beautiful Mind

. . . .

"When your mind awakens, your life comes alive and the creative adventure of your soul takes off."
JOHN O'DONOHUE

It was hour three of strolling through the sixth arrondissement in Paris's Saint-Germain-des-Prés neighborhood, and something within me was terribly *off*.

I was immersed in a city I absolutely adored, surrounded by beauty in all its forms: stunning fashion; colorful fruits, vegetables, and flowers in market stalls; breathtaking architecture;

artful displays in every storefront; and acres of magnificent green spaces and parks. And while I was certainly lifted by every aspect of the sensory input rushing into my body, I felt a soul-based dissonance that worried me. What could possibly be wrong *here*?

I had grown accustomed to feeling out of whack back home, where my entire life was still smoldering from the flames of divorce and financial meltdown. It was understandable to not be on my game as I was still recovering from my nuclear winter.

But hadn't I escaped the bonds of all that held me imprisoned by crossing the proverbial pond and putting 4,500 miles between that life and Paris?

Even though I had done a masterful job of changing my external landscape, I had neglected mightily the work on my inner landscape. And when the two worlds met, the jarring vibration felt like a cacophonous piano chord cutting through my brain.

Sitting alone in a bustling bistro, I refused to believe I could not recraft my experience of life and felt even more determined to set myself free.

I slid my espresso cup over to the side of the little round table and began mapping out in my journal the current state of affairs inside my mind. It was an attic of dark corners, dusty shelving packed full of things I no longer wanted or needed, and boxes upon boxes taped tightly shut with all their contents hidden away.

I took a deep breath and cut into the first box. Just a bunch of old stuff. Nothing scary, just thought clutter I no longer had any use for. Not so bad! I could just jettison that box entirely. Heartened, I moved to the second box and opened it.

Uh-oh.

That one was a viper pit of autopilot behaviors (numbing out, overworking, withholding joy and fun from myself, and staying in a state of looping anxiety) that kept me stuck, resentful, in a blaming posture, unhealthy, and separated from what I was craving the most: a lightness of being. I rooted around and saw film clips of painful memories I had unknowingly carried for years. I had never let that suffering fully land, let alone heal, as I was always in red-alert motion and in self-distracting mode.

As dusk fell around me and the lights of Paris illuminated the city, I completed my attic inventory. I surveyed the room, with all of its contents now divided into two categories: leave behind and create anew. I left the old behaviors and thinking that had once kept me glued to a life I did not want in an unceremonious tower against the wall. I vowed to never pick up one item from that poisonous pile again. The "create anew" box was small, so I tucked it under my arm, turned off the light, and said goodbye to that space forever.

Back on the street, I felt a shift begin to loosen the tightness in my mood and soul. The contents of the little box from the attic rattled around a bit as I moved, and I was careful not to jostle them too much. I peeked inside the box every now and then as I made my way to my hotel and found the interior hospitable and welcoming to scrutiny.

The following morning, I walked along the Seine and eased myself into the majesty that is the Musée d'Orsay. After touring each floor and luxuriating in each sumptuous piece, I walked past the museum's restaurant and nearly lost my mind.

I was transfixed. The space was one of the most beautiful interiors I had ever seen. Towering, arched windows filled the room with natural light. Ornate, traditional French decor, light fixtures, and sculptures lifted my eyes and heart up, up, up. And then there were the surprising, fun dining room chairs, little contemporary works of art punctuating the room with joie de vivre.

As I stood and stared, I knew that my work was to fashion an interior landscape as lovely and lustrous as that room. To bring vibrancy, shine, and renewal to the contents of the small box I had retrieved from the attic of me. To start over with a fresh approach, an entirely new way of being and thinking.

I knew I would need to become a more skilled curator for my mind, no longer casually letting things take up space on the shelves within me. I would only bring in what I met with a discerning eye and careful consideration.

I turned to leave and spotted a small gallery that I had somehow missed, tucked off the side of the building. I leaned into the room to scout it out and was drawn to a painting on the far-left wall. I walked toward it in reverence, held fast in an electric trance, feeling pieces of concrete shake loose here and there. Each step left behind old bits of me that no longer served. The edges of my vision darkened, and the room elongated as if it were stretched Silly Putty.

Two women stood in front of the painting. One turned and looked up at me as I approached. I must have worn on my face what I felt was happening inside my body. She touched her friend's forearm to signal to her to move aside. I smiled a thank you to her and turned toward the work.

The painting, *La Solitude* by Thomas Alexander Harrison, depicts a woman standing in a rowboat. She's turned away from us, facing outward, searching. Thinking. The woman and the boat are bright, illuminated from overhead, while the remainder of the canvas is mostly dark. It is a work of calm exploration and discovery. Confidence in soaking in the truth, beauty, and connection to inner and outer worlds that can sometimes be touched only in moments of solitude. The traveler, the seeker, the creator, the dreamer with just enough light to find her way. Guided by the horizon's edge to move forward in a world that has grown dark.

A message in a bottle from the artist. He had reached across time to tell me of his dreams and the soulful solitude that fueled him. It was a message that transcended time and space, like the light we see from stars already dead.

One more chunk of concrete hit the floor. Without taking my eyes off the woman in the boat, I blindly reached around in my purse for a tissue to dry my eyes and face. A pressure inside my chest built and opened like an accordion within my ribcage. When it rose to my throat, I could name it. Something I had not felt for years. I had almost forgotten its dewy sweetness. Hope.

The painting was a salve for my ragged soul. It promised me that I already had everything I needed for the next part of my journey. That I could withstand loss and grief and transmute the entire swirling mess into something beautiful. I could cross the waters of uncertainty and fear and find a new frontier of being in the world with nothing held back.

While in the moment I didn't know exactly how to make that happen, Paris had gifted me potent clues for what would get me closer to inner radiance and the ability to soften into remembering what I craved. I intuited that it had something to do with moving the body so that the mind rests and allows stillness; that it is important to open up and place ourselves in front of beauty, see with new eyes, and curate a beautiful mind.

I did know, though, that this magic was all tied to what Paulo Coelho calls "inspiration." Breathing in the oxygen of everything that brings us alive with flames of passion. Excitement. A desire to connect in novel ways with our interior chambers. The stacking of the blocks of art, rest, and experiences to construct towers of alchemical transformations.

Inspiration is the very same divine vigor that drives our creativity, unleashing the power deep within us up through the membranes that protect us and out into the world. With its

"Go get yourself and be ready to meet what is."

Rev. angel Kyodo williams

exploratory nature, it leads us ultimately toward the discovery of new lands.

How do we become better cultivators and protectors of the energy of inspiration—the elusive force that transmutes nothing into something as if it were touched by the wizard's wand? How can we foster the development and health of a pipeline of such energy, so that it is available to us the moment we reach for it?

I asked myself these questions as I walked the streets of Paris back toward my hotel. Further, just as I had discovered during my imaginative trip to the attic of my mind, what do we need to leave behind that no longer serves us (or perhaps never did)? What do we need to create anew? And how do we figure out how to do these things?

Over the course of several years, through trial and error, I pieced together the recipe, a deceptively simple treasure map that is as fun to follow as it is to reach our desired destination. It's a map I call The 5MS.

Inspiration's Foundation: The 5MS

The small vein on Jen's forehead pulsated in anger and frustration. "You're joking," she scoffed.

"Nope. I promise it's magic," I said.

She leaned back in her chair and glared at me. "You remember that I came to you for help with building revenue, right? And figuring out my marketing and setting a strategy for the next year? Look, I appreciate this gorgeous bag and all of the creativity supplies. Really, I do. But honestly, I don't have time for playing around."

I used to be Jen, and I recognized her irritation, fear, and exhaustion. Her desperation to fix her business and make it rain. Her desire for me to cut to the chase, tell her what was going to be on the test, and coach her with the answers.

She absolutely did not want to hear about inspiration. "I'm in a sea of alligators, Susie," she said. "DEFCON 1, ya know? Razor-thin margins, competitors everywhere, and zero client loyalty that *I swear* is gonna put me in an early grave." Jen paused for a moment and tapped the table with the back of the colossal ring on her forefinger and then bore her eyes into mine. "Everybody wants double the work for half the price. Expectations you cannot meet. Jesus . . . I'm so tired."

I opened my mouth to speak, but Jen leapt ahead of me.

"I used to be the belle of this fucking ball," she said. "Clients clamoring for my work. Clients who saw and valued my talent. What the hell happened? How did I lose my mojo?"

What Jen did not yet realize was that her inability to command top rates and attract ideal clients was inexorably tied to her depleted fund of inspiration. She had long stopped putting quality input into the mechanism of her mind and soul. When she turned the faucet of her creativity to "on," the once powerful current was now barely dripping. Clients sensed her overwhelm and the disarray of her personal life, her thinking. She rushed calls and talked over people. She averted her gaze from what clients really needed and focused only on closing sales. The harder she pushed, the more her revenue and reputation retreated.

I told her an abbreviated version of my story and what had turned everything around for me. I coaxed her into giving my coaching methodology a chance. At last, she agreed.

When we met again in a cafe several weeks later, she bounded over to me and hugged me. She tucked my arm inside hers and said, "I've got us a table in the back. You are not going to believe what I have to tell you."

I already knew what she was going to tell me. Not the specifics, but the gist of her story.

"Sit here," she said, tapping the chair facing the window. She brushed her curly brown hair from her eyes and took a deep breath. "It's so good. Wait till you hear."

I settled in, feeling like a child at story time. All ears.

"First," she said, "you were right." She recalled the homework assignment I had given her—doing The 5Ms each day: Meditation, Morning Pages, Movement, Moments of Inspired Learning, and Making Something.

I CAME UP with the idea of The 5Ms (well, four of them) during one of my daily walks. I had been happily lost in thought for well over an hour as I hiked deeper and deeper into the Nantahala National Forest. As I watched sunlight reflect off slices of mica on the trail, I inhaled the cinnamon-hay odor of late summer soil and snacked on the zingy ideas that landed every few feet. In these woods, I did my best thinking. Or no thinking. In that between-world where there were no distractions, no limiting beliefs folding my sense of self in half, I could tune into a divine transmitter that churned out pages like an old mimeograph machine. Insights, connecting dots, new questions, resolutions to troubling challenges, and surges of confidence came in rolling waves.

"What is it about writing Morning Pages and moving my body?" I asked the white oaks, pines, and tulip poplars. "How is it they both transport me no matter my state of mind when I begin? And there's another M, meditation. Same thing. Each offers a way through the clutter to the other side, where the challenge solves itself. The boat rights its course. Each M helps me darn the tiny holes caused by snags on the goings-on and limiting beliefs of the previous day, before they tear the fabric of me to unrecognizable threads."

I continued my hike, feeling satisfied with the day's catch from the sea of inspiration. To celebrate, I pulled up an audio file I had saved on my phone. I stood in the middle of the trail, letting my dog, Sophie, nose around and explore, closed my eyes, and listened to Mary Oliver read her poem "Wild Geese." Her reassuring voice, like an unconditionally loving fairy godmother sent to save us from the piercing dread that we'll never be quite good enough, traveled up and down the spine of my sense of self. In a little over one minute, I felt her words realigning me, helping me remember that I would find my place in the world. As the last line of her poem echoed inside of me, I understood the fourth M: Moments of Inspired Learning.

I had 4MS. The fifth, Making Something, came a week later when I was stirring a bubbling puttanesca sauce and dropping in fresh, fragrant basil plucked from the plant on my windowsill. As my wooden spoon made little currents, the sauce gurgled and popped, releasing whiffs of garlic and oregano. I stirred and dropped into a standing meditation, transported to the place I go on long drives, a zone of both awareness and unawareness. Gentle hand movements in the act of creating conducted my subconscious mind forward and pushed my heated, "doing" brain to the background. Soon I would mix in a bit of pasta water and al dente rigatoni before plating my masterpiece. I tapped the spoon on the side of the pan and knew that Making Something had to join the quartet of liberating actions that sets us free.

Here, then, are The 5MS:

1 **Meditation.** Before your obstinate inner critic begins to bark that there is no way you can or will meditate, I can offer some easy suggestions. Start with five minutes of simply sitting quietly. Even if all kinds of thoughts pop to the surface, just let them come, and notice them. You do not have to stop having thoughts. Just don't try to force them away, because the more you resist what is going on in your mind, the more your jumpy thoughts will persist. There are also myriad options online for

free guided meditations. Try a few of those and see what you think. Eventually, you can work up to twenty minutes or more each morning. I do a variety of different meditations, some guided, some not. Explore a bit and find your own fit. You will be surprised by how gifting yourself a little time to simply relish quiet and stillness will work on your rough edges like a fine-grit, spiritual sandpaper.

2 **Morning Pages.** The brainchild of author Julia Cameron, Morning Pages are three pages written in longhand each day. As their name suggests, you do them in the morning. They are your private depository of all your crazy-making thoughts, a daily brain dump onto the page. This simple practice holds immense magic and is powerfully effective. Getting all of the mumbo jumbo out of your brain—all the whining, rants, fears, frustrations, and celebrations—truly helps free your mind for creating. Morning Pages incinerate any thought hangovers that hold me trapped. They help me keep only the thoughts that are uplifting and fuel me forward.

3 **Movement.** For me, this is an hour of physical exercise, typically hiking with Sophie. If you need to start with thirty minutes, do so. Unlike Morning Pages, you can get your Movement time in at any point of the day. Experiment to see what time works best for you. Try to immerse yourself in silence and resist the urge to make this time "productive." Avoid taking calls or checking email or distracting yourself with other voices until you have had enough time to hear your own voice first. Always bring a small journal that will fit inside your pocket and a pen. You will find this time is one of your best idea-generating windows of the day.

4 **Moments of Inspired Learning.** These fill us back up after the first three Ms have worked their magic emptying us out.

We can choose our most precious and quenching Moments of Inspired Learning each day. They are cloudbursts of rainwater into the dry wells that live within us when we move for too long in the desert heat of overdoing. Let go of the rigid idea that your Moments of Inspired Learning have to be time-consuming. As you can see from my moment with Mary Oliver, a little over one minute was all the time I needed.

There is another powerful aspect of Moments of Inspired Learning: they foster connection to our imagination and intuition and create a sense of community with both the creator of the content and all others who are consuming it. We can feel a sense of camaraderie within the giant circle of fellow travelers and seekers and take comfort in their company.

5 **Making Something.** This is as straightforward as it sounds. Keep some markers, colored pencils, paints, and your journal handy—you might doodle, sketch, color, or paint. You may opt to cook something or play around with a puzzle.

I'll pause here for just a moment while I let you have a hissy fit. Scoff! Cry out that I'm full of baloney! Get out all your limiting beliefs about art-making and creating so that you can focus on and take in what I am saying.

Let's see if I have guessed some of the thoughts that have galloped through your mind over the last thirty seconds:

- "Who has time for such silliness?"
- "There's no way I can do anything remotely artistic."
- "What is this? Preschool?"
- "Do you have any idea how busy I am?"
- "Please tell me how this is even slightly helpful for me or my business."

All well and good. No harm in letting the ol' monkey mind have a good screeching session. Breathe in deeply now and exhale. Sit up straight and listen without judgment.

Making Something is your VIP pass to your creativity back channels, which are often hidden reserves—treasure chests—filled with golden ideas, sparkling jewels of intuition and insight, guiding us to profound pattern recognition and dot connecting. We will discuss this phenomenon more deeply in chapter 3, but for now, understand the Willy Wonka Golden Ticket nature of Making Something. Even if you do not fully believe me yet, hold it with a light grasp as a possibility.

The key to Making Something is to get your hands moving without attachment to the finished product. This can be as brief as a ten-minute session or as long as you like. Repetition is more important than session length, so it is better to do ten minutes every day than seventy minutes once a week. We need to keep returning to the practice. Face the resistance and pierce the veil of avoidance. Get in there and go. In so doing, we are telling the mind and our sense of self that we are people who show up, who keep our promises. That we are deserving of and expecting flow and ease.

It is in the throes of Making Something that we discover the calm of collage, the satisfying squeezing of clay, the curious dance of light and shadow, and the blank page that is equal parts enchanting and terrifying. We'll ride the rapids of discovering all kinds of fun creativity tools and gear. Creamy pencils that we sharpen by bursts of rotations, watching peels curl into the chamber of the sharpener. Waxy crayons. Powdery pastels that leave our fingers as colorful as our art. Vibrant paints, thick with possibility. Watercolors that dance on wet paper and blend into new shapes before our eyes. The pleasing tactile nature of graphite on a smooth page in our journal. The call and response of making marks that puts us in a trance. The experience of our hand moving across the page.

Making Something is unlike anything else we do. It stands alone in its singular, playful power to lift, center, and empower us. It stokes the fire that inflates the balloon of us, hoisting our back-channel basket of creativity over landscapes we did not know even existed. It connects us with what brings us alive. It takes us to "beginner's mind"—the rich, childlike zone of exploring what could be while seeing with new eyes. By keeping us solidly in the present moment, making helps us feel and know that right now, everything is okay. We are okay. It gives us just enough daylight to illuminate our way forward in a day or season of darkness.

I find that when I begin my day by engaging in even just a few minutes of making, the dominoes of the day tend to fall as I intend without so much effort required on my part. Tiny ideas become bolder and more willing to appear too.

"SO, YEAH, meditation," Jen said. "At first, I couldn't sit still. I was so frustrated that thought-crawls kept running across my mind. Relentless. It took me a week before I could actually sit in quiet for five minutes. I'm up to ten minutes now. Even if I didn't do any of the other Ms, this alone has shifted how I feel."

She went on. "Morning Pages are easy-peasy. These have been the simplest change for me. I guess because it feels like a school assignment that I can master." She laughed. "You know what's scary, though? All the crap I was carrying around all day, every day. Some days, I just write three pages of sheer bitching. I can totally see how my thoughts have held me back and kept me super stuck."

"What did you choose to do for Movement?" I asked.

"Oh my God! I cannot believe how much I have missed moving my body. What's it been, five years since I did yoga consistently? It used to be such an integral part of my life. Why did I even stop? Anyway, this is gold too. I feel so much stronger. Limber. Centered in my body."

Jen continued. "You're gonna laugh. For my Moments of Inspiration, I have about a year's worth of audiobooks queued up to listen to on my drive to the office. I have no idea why I have chosen to suffer during my commute, rerunning old conversations through my head that make me feel bad. I realized I've been reliving past arguments, even times when I felt supremely gaslighted, over and over during my time in the car. Super healthy, huh?"

"What are you listening to right now?" I asked.

"Frankl's *Man's Search for Meaning*."

"Oooh, excellent choice," I said.

"Every single thing I have been whining about looks completely ridiculous as I listen to his book. Talk about perspective! I have nothing to complain about. He just kept on going. Kept faith. So inspiring and humbling."

"How did you do with Making Something?" I asked.

Jen wrinkled her nose. "Not my strong suit, admittedly," she said. "I am still having trouble wrestling with the belief that whatever I make has to be *good*. Worthy of showing off. So I just got some markers and started doodling in the sketchbook you gave me. Five minutes of mindless doodling. I do like playing with colors without worrying about making a finished product. I'm starting to get what you call idea blurts too. Maybe at some point, I'll graduate to something more adventurous, like sketching."

"This is terrific! I'm thrilled that—"

"*Oh, yeah!* I forgot!" Jen interrupted. "Even though I have added things into my day, it's like I have more time. How is that even possible? And you know, I think I want to shift gears in my business. I've got some exciting ideas for things I'd like to change."

Bingo.

On the other side of stuck energy lie flow and freedom. On the other side of fear lies creativity. The 5MS are rocket fuel for inspiration and help us weave threads of success throughout each day by filling our near and far periphery with clarity, calm, jump-started insights, focus, and flow, as well as moments of joy.

Nearly four months after Jen began incorporating The 5Ms into her life, she returned to her former status of being the belle of the ball in her field of expertise. Rested, clear, confident, and reconnected to her creativity, her energy and messaging to clients landed powerfully. She enjoyed sorting and filtering client opportunities, selecting only the projects that excited her, working only with the clients who saw and valued her unique talent.

She was no longer chasing business, cutting her rates, or competing on price. She was back in charge of her life, her enterprise, her sense of self. Perhaps most importantly, she felt calm, joyful, and empowered, knowing now the formula for obtaining success and ease.

Make a plan right now to add The 5Ms into your day. Go into your planner and select a week within the next month to begin. Choose a week without too many obligations so that you may gently fold in your new habits and give them space to take root.

Like Jen and me, you'll soon discover their magic.

As you begin doing The 5Ms, you will develop the handy skill of being able to see around corners when in creative funks. Each of the five practices helps to dislodge old sludge within the veins of our thinking, beliefs, and actions. We stop resisting doing the work. We begin to believe we can create what it is we want to have happen. We step forward instead of hiding. We move through the old art scars and unhealthy habits that have been holding us back. We feel the power and fun of getting going. We notice as we accumulate days doing each practice; how the wizardry works on us, changes us, shapes our perspective in little and big ways, and guides us into and through our becoming.

The Open Focus of a Creator

"Just be here—really be here, with all five senses and no thought of anywhere else—and then let your meta-self move you."
MARTHA BECK

There's a gravel road in Clear Creek, a neighborhood on the outskirts of Highlands, North Carolina, that winds for miles through US Forest Service land. I've walked that road in every season, every sort of weather, for more than thirty years. I have thought through and made thousands of decisions and choices while tromping along the towering pines and deciduous trees, cycling through buds, lush foliage, brilliant colors, and naked branches.

I chose to leave the world of nonprofit leadership and become a real estate broker on that road. I have read aloud, with the trees as my audience, speeches for a graduation, an academic banquet, company retreats, and judges deciding custody of my stepchildren. While walking that road, I decided to get married, and then divorced.

I took my newborn son in a front-facing pouch, and later in a backpack while he played with my hair, for long, chatty walks. I mourned the loss of my father, doubled over in sobs, hands on knees. I have watched Sophie become joy incarnate, splashing in swimming holes or running like the wind.

I began birthing this book, stopping to scribble notes, line by line, mile by mile, on that road.

Each walk begins with my reciting gratitude out loud. The poplars, oaks, and maples stand like kind and wise ancestors, bending toward me to listen closely. I celebrate with them, and they nod their tops in rustling breezes. I meditate with eyes and heart wide open, step by step. Turn by turn.

I play games of manifesting to see if I can bring to my attention something surprising. Unexpected. A signal from the Universe that I am in partnership with all of creation and can dissolve into an energy that resonates with another unseen world, and call something forward into three-dimensional matter. I've done it dozens of times. Orange butterfly. Heart-shaped stone. A deer. A wild pink lady's slipper. An owl. A ruby red garnet the size of a pea. I always know when I'm "there"— in that blissful, buoyant state of receivership. Open. When I'm not bullshitting myself. When I've put down the petty concerns of daily life. When I'm 100 percent connected to the divine within me and all around me.

Some days, I slide into that delicious state without effort. That's when I'm like a woman in a white surveillance van, parked just down the street, wearing headphones and listening intently to pick up any signals or syllables.

What comes through in those times are Class 5 idea rapids. Kayaking on the whitecaps, paddling like crazy, I'm carried around rocks and overhanging branches. Ducking. Twisting. Forward. A small journal, tucked into a leather cover, a pencil, and I are engaged in a flurry of getting it all down.

The open focus of a creator. This state is, without a doubt, one of our most precious commodities for loving life in consonant vibration with every living thing, most notably ourselves. From this ledge, we have a twenty-twenty grasp of our point of view.

For entrepreneurs and creators, our point of view is the mirepoix base of our secret sauce. The vision, voice, perspective, and unique genius that make us who we are. Like no one else. This is what calls our audience, our clients, our community, right to us. Our sexy siren song that we play simply by living in accord with our true selves. This is the ethereal realm of the deepest connection we can experience. It is the origin of creative worlds powered by our unique fingerprints.

It is an inside-out job. And we cannot get there if we are spending too much time looking at what everyone else is doing and saying, obsessed with the notion that everyone except us has it all figured out. Wielding a stick to measure our progress and worth and convince ourselves of how far short we fall.

Here, we are trapped in the hideous pursuit of compare and despair that is the kill switch on our sense of self and our ability to connect with our intuition. Here, we are stopped from receiving juicy intel and insights that can only be born within the stock of our cauldron. Remember: When we are disconnected from ourselves, our efforts to connect with the market falter, sputter, and drop.

How might you open the aperture of who you are? Where do you need to turn your attention away from others so that you can see what only you can see? What can we fashion from the images that appear only to us? And why should we bother?

When we have the open focus of a creator, we are more optimistic, which ushers in our ability to see more possibilities, creativity's raw material and driving force. We muster up courage to make bold moves in our work and lives. We refuse to stall out and stay stuck. We discern and decide, letting our choices power our creativity with a confidence born of focusing on what we love. We more easily find meaning and enjoy feelings of fulfillment, a greater engagement with the world, and access to success.

The ability to hear ourselves think is a sacred and rare superpower. When we get out of the clamor, we can come to know what is and is not us. When we turn away from the din on our screens, we can feel and tap into the verdant void of silence and stillness. The quiet and calm are unnerving at first, but if we recognize we are merely reacting to old habits of distraction, we can settle into this new state.

Open focus provides us with an expansive state of being that bends time and coaxes us across the threshold from clinging control to empowered self-trust. Once through this portal, we inhabit a world of momentum, working with a tempo kept by the drumbeat of us. Energized and expectant of serendipity, we seek and find what our minds believe to be true and create what only we can create.

Creativity Space

"I like walking because it is slow, and I suspect that the mind, like the feet, works at about three miles an hour. If this is so, then modern life is moving faster than the speed of thought or thoughtfulness."

REBECCA SOLNIT

I grew up in the '70s, in a remote town of 2,500 people. We had one channel, Channel 4, and more times than not, the reception was too poor to really watch anything. I remember standing in front of our television, hand on the antenna rotor. I would turn the dial to the left, waiting for it to slowly grind toward the "W" on the dial face.

"How 'bout now? Any better?" I'd ask my brother and sister on the sofa.

"No," they'd groan.

I'd try turning the dial to the right and would wait again.

"Let's try east."

When our patience with trying various directions of the antenna wore thin, we'd give up and find something else to do. Most of the time, I'd head outside to the yard or the woods.

A large, domed rock in the backyard generally served as home plate when we played baseball. The flat cap of the rock jutted out of the soil and provided a wonderful perch for quiet contemplation and daydreaming.

I'd sit on "home plate" for hours, pulling up individual strands of grass and rolling them through my fingers. I'd place the blade lengthwise between my hands and blow into my hands across the grass, like an instrument reed. I became proficient at making different pitches and calls.

I'd watch ants busying themselves in miniature ant hills, Japanese beetles making little towers of themselves like circus acrobats, and bumblebees hovering around purple clover pom-poms. Robins, cardinals, and towhees sang and called to each other from the woods behind me.

Hours would pass, and by the time I was called to dinner, I had gone on several make-believe adventures and had many imagined conversations. I had also spent long stretches not thinking of anything at all in particular. I'd just let my thoughts lift up and out of the top of my head like bubbles.

I was gifted with an older sister who lived in her imagination as much as I did. We'd play together and create a different world each day, or we'd choose to go our own way and drop into our fantasies solo. And even though I was afraid of almost everything and everyone as a child, I was supremely joyful, playful, and peaceful. My imagined world, my world of deep contemplation, always transported me to a zone of comfort, excitement, and curious wonder.

As an adult, I continue to love this kind of escape into imagination and mind-wandering. Not only do I find it as soul nourishing and enjoyable as I did as a child, but I also know time spent without any thought agenda is one of my greatest sources of creativity and ideation. No specific problems to solve, worries to wrestle, or tasks to prioritize and then check off lists. Just delicious, long stretches of daydreaming.

Allowing creativity space fills the well and keeps us aware and present. Gentle and slower pacing for our feverish frontal lobes lets inklings surface and become leggy, awkward idea teenagers. Thoughts may spin around like Bambi on the ice and ultimately fade. Or they may take on a robust energy and develop into your next big idea.

Think about this past week. How much time did you allow yourself in pure, seemingly unproductive mind wandering? Did you gift your brain a daydream or two? How often did you let your mind get lost on purpose?

When I go to the woods in the spring, I search for wild irises along the banks of small creeks. Their hearty cleverness and effortless beauty are just the tonics I need. The wild iris knows enough to plant itself near water and in acidic soil, giving its roots, leaves, and perfect, blue stars of petals the ideal conditions for it to flourish.

Our creative courage has similar requirements. We need to place ourselves near the source of our inspiration, be that in nature, a favorite chair, a quiet library, a vibrant art museum, or a bustling cafe. When we scooch up to the heat of our creativity, we can recognize that the desire to pull away is our signal we are onto something. And we can choose to feel the fear all the way through, stay with it, and then witness its leaving. We can vow to stay in our seat no matter how edgy and nervous we feel.

Before I turn back toward home, I stand on a creek bank and watch the water move without effort over and around mossy rocks. I know in an instant my job, our job, is to be like water when in the creative thrash. Coursing forward with joyful enthusiasm, flowing around obstacles, and never stopping.

There's a soft chair, a park bench, or a grassy patch under a tree that is calling. Open up some space for synapses to fire in random order. Drop into no past, no present, no future. Consider going for a stroll through a bustling city square. Saunter along the edge of a quaint port, or immerse yourself in the hush of a snowy, solo walk. Soothe your cramped and over-thinking mind with an adventure without an agenda or a destination. Go nowhere and everywhere, and let your creativity have some sunshine, oxygen, and room to grow.

My Shack in Woodstock

"I went up to Woodstock and just read, and read, and read, and read, for five years."
JOSEPH CAMPBELL

I think about Joseph Campbell almost every day. The first time I read his explanation of the hero's journey, I was sitting on the floor in front of the fire, propped up against the sofa. I understood immediately the power of his template of the monomyth, which reveals how each of us goes about the business of deep transformation and living the adventure that is our life. I stared down at the wrinkled paperback, blinking tears onto the pages. I felt as if an angel had come to sit beside me and whisper secrets in my ear. Secrets I was desperate to hear.

Beyond the comfort of now having a map to guide me and provide context for where I was on my own journey, I finally understood how I am built. I discovered why it is I am attracted to pursuing certain experiences, pushing myself well beyond what I think I am capable of, so that I may bring something back that I discovered in the depths of a cave, while battling what Campbell would call my dragon, and offer it to someone who might find it useful.

Right along with the soul-washing relief of possessing this secret to living fully, I knew that so much more was required of me to deliver on the promise locked within me. And not unlike one of Campbell's heroines, I refused the call by turning away from my potential for years.

Ultimately, I reached a point when the pain of refusing the call was greater than my fear. It took the Great Recession, as well as the end of my marriage, to provide me with a taser arc of awareness that shocked me forward across the threshold.

Over the last decade, I have embarked on and completed dozens of heroine's journeys (or as I call them, Creative Rebel's Voyages). Each adventure dislodges mental and emotional concrete that once held me fused and imprisoned. More heavy, gray chunks fall to the ground into clouds of dust. Each journey brings release, paring me down, more and more, to the bones of my true self.

As delighted as I was with my gradual return to my true nature, I realized that the years of stress, paltry sleep, consuming mountains of digital content, and an addiction to all work and no play had rewired my brain. Sitting down and concentrating for any length of time made me antsy. When I tried to read anything other than brief snippets here and there, my attention scattered. Each time I tried to refocus on the page, my eyes would glaze over and my brain would collapse like a failed soufflé. This was completely unnerving for someone who used to read for hours in yawning, uninterrupted stretches, who got lost in books with full attention and delight.

I turned to Joseph Campbell for guidance. When he found himself jobless at the age of twenty-five during the Great Depression, Campbell took the little money he had saved and withdrew to a rented shack in Woodstock, New York. There, he devoted nine or so hours every day to reading. He would later describe these five years as the "most important period of my scholarship and study."

So one winter, I packed up a box of books and drove to the beach in Florida with Sophie. Each day, like Campbell, I read and read and read. When I returned to Highlands a month later,

"Sustained aloneness brings you to a tipping point where the pendulum of life returns you to others."

Stephen Batchelor

I joyfully continued my monk-like practice of daily reading and writing.

Now, each morning, I wake up hours before dawn and begin my work. Morning writing and reading have become a deep spiritual practice for me, and as a result, a calm, profound joy has settled into my heart.

Initially, my body and mind fiercely resisted this focus. My brain had become addicted to abbreviated thinking, disconnected strands of ideas, and distraction. I craved everything and anything that would push me out of my centered zone of what bestselling author and professor Cal Newport calls "deep work." The harder my addiction to distraction pushed forward, the more determined I became to hold my ground.

Once I was finally able to hear myself think, I knew just how much I missed that smart, wildly curious woman whose brain snacked on intellectual and spiritual puzzles. I also knew how far I had distanced myself from the young girl who used to let herself be transported by beautiful prose and compelling ideas. I wanted her back, and I chose to defend her rebirth with every choice, every decision, every day.

After cementing this habit, I can attest to the incredible magic that is now afoot in my life. Honestly, some days, the raw power of it threatens to completely push me under. There's an inner tug-of-war between my former self and the one crawling out of the chrysalis. I keep an observer's watch, from a solitary post in a lighthouse, scanning the horizon for brewing storms. I have to recommit every morning.

Not unlike divergence and convergence, the accordion of the Creative Rebel's Voyage frames the opportunity for us to leave, fan out as widely as possible, get lost on purpose, consolidate our insights, and reconnect and share generously with our community. There will always be plenty of darkness to transcend, and more than enough light to find our footing in the cave of our own personal dragon.

Solitude nourishes my creativity and cells. It fills my lungs and opens me, petal by petal, toward the sunlight. I am at my best when I have had my introvert's tank replenished with no other agenda or inquiry other than those I have created. Once filled, I have something to offer the world and am eager to engage fully, completely.

Solitude returns us to inhabiting the world with a full-body presence. It is a haven against the crowded and noisy world. A defense against others' energies that threaten to drain your own.

Run your 5Ms on the solar power of solitude. Bolster your inspiration by working in periods of quiet, in long stretches of no mind, no time. Leave yourself alone to hear your own undiluted thinking, to feel the edges of you once more, knowing where you begin and end, what is you, what is the world.

Return to the circle and offer what you've found. Empty your drawstring leather pouch at your feet and let everyone root around in all you have found to be fascinating, curious, beautiful, worthy of further study, heartbreaking.

exercise Finding Your Shack in Woodstock

What is your shack in Woodstock? That is, where is it that you need to retreat, in mind and body, to recover the version of you that might have long disappeared? What does it take for you to do your best work? And what are you willing to subtract from your daily life to make that happen?

Write down your thoughts in your journal. Next, plan a solo retreat, great or small, that will provide you with perspective, rest, and rejuvenation. This retreat could be as simple as three hours by yourself in a local cafe or as elaborate as a week (or more!) spent on your own in an inspirational setting.

inspiration beacon

IF YOU let yourself get still for just a moment or two, you will hear the call to adventure. It will rise above the din, land in your ears, and fill you with equal parts excitement and fear. Pick up your backpack and turn toward the sun.

3

Accessing Your Creativity Back Channels

(By Bringing Yourself Alive)

"People say that what we're all seeking is a meaning for life. I think that what we're seeking is an experience of being alive."

JOSEPH CAMPBELL

EVER SINCE I had a brief conversation with cartoonist, author, and teacher Lynda Barry on the 1440 Multiversity campus in Scotts Valley, California, about what she means about the power of an image, I have wrestled with understanding what "image" means and how it works on us. Image is connected to the moving of our hands, which drops us into a trance that gives us access to our vast, often untapped creativity that we wouldn't otherwise have access to—what Lynda calls "back of mind," and what I call our creativity back channels.

I have come to define "image" as anything that evokes emotion, memory, meaning, or connection. It is the power outlet, the plug, and the electricity all at once. It is what is happening to us when we are making something—bringing it into being. Bringing it to life.

I see the power of an image as a current. When we create and allow that current to flow through us, from us, it enlivens us, awakens us, opens us. If we choose to share our creations, that stream of energy travels to others, connecting us in bonds that defy time and space.

Given our tendency to overdo, push ourselves to exhaustion, and practice distraction, our unique creativity back channels are a place that we, as entrepreneurs and small business owners (and creators), rarely ever access. In all our clamoring for more productivity, ironically, we hold at bay our ability to intuit the wisest path forward for us and our entrepreneurial efforts. As a result, we don't see that the exact right problem solving, the one that fits us, is on our own terms.

For example, let's say you are wrestling with just how to market your products and/or services or launch something new. So, you take a look around at how other entrepreneurs in your field are doing their marketing, and every line of copy, every approach, every funnel, every aspect of their campaigns . . . it all fills you with dread and aversion. The "experts" say theirs is the tried-and-true approach. No matter how much you try to emulate them, though, your body and mind are locked, frozen in a "*hell no*" stance. You delay. You decide you just don't like marketing. You wonder if you are even cut out for this entrepreneurial gig after all.

But you don't have a marketing problem. You have a temporary inability to access your creativity back channels. Access your back channels and you access the singular voice, energy, and way of communicating within you that reaches and lands, no matter how crowded the computer screens in front of your ideal client, or how limited the bandwidth of your desired audience.

When you ideate and create from your back channels, you do so on your terms; what resonates is in alignment with you, born of your creative seat of power and ease.

Before you decide this all sounds too mysterious and impossible for you, note that you have already been accessing your back channels. This came naturally to you as a child when you played, or every time you joyfully approached a challenge or project with "beginner's mind." You do it every time you have an intuitive hit (which we tend to either ignore or override). You access your back channels when you let your mind wander, your body rest, and your hands move. When you put yourself in front of beauty, let a poem wash over you, make a quick sketch, visit an art gallery, attend a show, tour a botanical garden, or journal on a quiet morning.

Accessing your back channels is not just a nice or fun thing to do. It holds the key to turning your business around and solving any problem that comes your way. When we access our back channels, we enter into an energetic conversation with the deepest parts of ourselves and others. An inner exchange and a contribution to the world's frequency that feels euphoric to both give and receive.

This is the state of existence that Joseph Campbell would say we are all seeking: the rapture of being alive. And this is why creativity holds such transformative powers for the one who is creating and the one receiving, taking in, the creativity of another.

The current finds the audience; the image lands. The energy exchange occurs. How we receive it is the power of our own image-making that shapes and interprets it through our personal experiences and emotions. It lands like water on a tender, new shoot of green, which the shoot then pulls up through its roots and sends it to where it is needed most.

Are we willing to open, to dive deeply within ourselves, to do the deep work to create images, and then release that voltage into the world, unsure where it will travel or where or how it will land, like a child pushing a toy boat from the edge of a pond?

Are we willing to create from our hearts, which are full of wonder, curiosity, and joy, as well as grief, fear, and loneliness?

Can we get going and get our hands moving as Lynda suggests?

We have the power to transcend the walls within us and around us. There is profound bliss in the meaning we receive, the meaning we ascribe, and the emotion and energy that comes through us, the creator, to the ones consuming it.

How do we get to that place of willingness to begin, to risk our sensitive hearts? And once we have managed to get started, how do we settle down the wild horse of us, who wants to buck and thrash, breaking us free from the confinement of staying in the work?

This chapter is an adventure in how to do exactly that, to give you direct access to the verdant back channels within you. We can take leave of our judging, analytical minds and cozy up to new frontiers of our creativity through sketching upside-down images; blind contour drawing; making big, bold, fat messes and gaining confidence in the doing; becoming a champion of the simple tools that set us free; and discovering our unique process of creation.

We are going to learn how to throw the hounds of the mind off the scent of our work so we can keep our hands moving and making. When we do, we reach not just a place of potential creativity and connection to self and others. There in the back channels, we exist, work, and communicate with our ideal clients in brand new ways. We solve the business problems that have vexed us. There, in that emotional, energetic exchange, we touch something and something touches us, a reciprocal sparking of the fuse of what brings us and our market alive.

exercise The Elephant in the Room

I remember wanting to stay in my zone of comfort, where I understood how the game was played, knew the rules, and knew how to win. The zone of my strategic intellect. And while that part of us is certainly one of the engines that can power us forward, it can only take us so far.

For us to know something anew, discover something novel, or connect with and create from our depths, getting beyond our analytical minds is the first job. Don't get me wrong, I love my powerful, strategic mind! But in order for me to create from new vision, to plumb the leagues of possibilities, I need to transcend that part of me and let my body take the wheel.

When we entrepreneurs find ourselves in unfamiliar waters, out of ideas, we can choose to loosen our reliance on our minds and instead lean into our bodies through art-making. We can only know how to be more creative by experiencing it. This is not an intellectual exercise. Let's give it a whirl!

Take out your journal and a pencil. We are going to do a drawing exercise inspired by art teacher Betty Edwards, author of *Drawing on the Right Side of the Brain*. Have a look at the elephant below. We are going to sketch this beauty.

I wish I could be a fly on the wall of your brain right now, eavesdropping on all those cries from your critical, analytical mind. Just for fun, write a few of those juicy comments down. Mine would be something like these:

- "What? You're kidding. You cannot draw that trunk."
- "Muscles? Ears? Nope."
- "Riiiight. You'll for sure nail how to draw those legs."

Notice how the mind loves to label according to what it knows, and to bob around in a sea of compare and despair? How limited you feel as a result; how defeated you are before you even get started. Anxiety is shutting off the lights in you, one by one.

Guess what? We are not going to draw that elephant. Instead, we are going to draw *this* elephant:

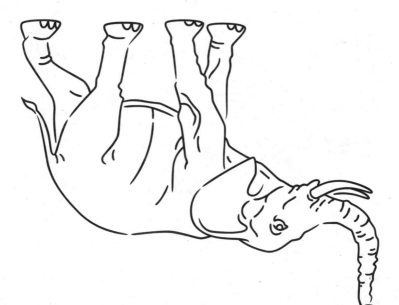

Ah. Now that's a little better. A bit of oxygen returned to the room, no? A tiny bit of possibility? Why, all of a sudden, does this seem more approachable?

Because the language part of us is muted now. This is no longer "an elephant you cannot draw." This is now simply a collection of marks on a white page. Much more accessible. This is our doorway in.

Let's focus only on connecting lines and curves. Select an area of the image and begin drawing. Keeping your eye on the image, let your pencil make marks on your page, moving from one part of the image to the next. Line, small curve, long curve, slope, dash here, dash there.

By drawing from an upside-down image, our censoring brain takes a nice little nap. It is no longer analyzing, criticizing, labeling. It's letting the copilot part of our brain do the heavy lifting.

When our brains are no longer focusing on trying to draw a known element such as an elephant's body, our inner critic quiets down. It no longer chirps that we do not have the skills for this. Rather, we simply go about the job of drawing lines and curves. This puts our brains into what Betty Edwards calls a "spatial, global processing" mode and away from "verbal, analytic processing."

As you draw, notice what is happening in your body. Can you lock in on that feeling? Stay in the net for a minute after you land. Remember that sensation

When you are finished, flip your image over and have a look. Are you surprised by how well you sketched after all? Well done! Do a dance around your desk! As fun and exciting as this is, the sketch is not the only, or even main, intended destination. Remember, the act of sketching is one key to the portal of creativity and innovation. (Of course, you may absolutely delight in seeing your finished sketch and be proud of it, too!)

exercise Blind Contour Drawing

Now that we are good and warmed up, let's try something a bit more adventurous: blind contour drawing. This is drawing without looking down at your paper. All you need is a pencil, your journal, and a subject. The trick to, and power of, blind contour drawing is that by focusing entirely on our subject, we flip a switch in our brain and are transported from a state of distraction, fear, perfectionism, and desire to control to one of presence, flow, ease, possibility, and power. Pretty nifty!

A special shout-out to all my control freak brothers and sisters. I know this exercise will light up your need-to-control buttons. Take heart. This time, we aren't the only weirdos in the room. *Everybody* struggles with this. As we will find out, our instinct to control during this exercise will pop up like a bunny out of its warren. Just expect it, breathe through it, and understand you are in most excellent company.

Author Sam Anderson describes the process this way:

> The goal of blind drawing is to really see the thing you're looking at, to almost merge with it spiritually, rather than retreat into your mental image of it. Our brains are designed to simplify—to reduce the tumult of the world into order. Blind drawing trains us to stare at the chaos, to honor it. It is an act of meditation, as much as it is an artistic practice—a gateway to pure being. It forces us to study the world as it actually is.
>
> Part of the magic of blind drawing is the impossibility of doing it wrong. This makes it the perfect antidote to perfectionism, because its first and only step is to abandon any hope of perfection. But inevitably, almost by accident, your

hand will produce little slivers of excellence—a nose that looks exactly right, an inscrutable expression on someone's face, the dip and curve of a dog's back—but then these will be obliterated, immediately, by the subsequent maelstrom of lines. I have learned to enjoy the feeling of swimming in sensory ignorance, to appreciate the vast distance between my hand and the reality it tries to trace.

Ready to give it a try? Take out your journal and a pencil. Select an image to draw. You could use a photograph out of a magazine or any item you have handy. Or you might even prop up a mirror and do a blind contour drawing of yourself! Once you have selected the image, make sure it is in full view and you are comfortably seated. Take a deep breath and exhale. Relax.

Fix your eyes on the outline of the item you are going to draw. It doesn't matter where you choose to start, just pick a spot. Place your pencil on the page. This is the last time you will look at your journal page until you complete the drawing.

Looking at the item, track its edge with your eyes while drawing the contour very slowly. Slowly. Slowly. We will want to race forward; notice that urge and ignore it. Continue in a steady, continuous line and do not lift your pencil from your paper.

There may be moments when you become disoriented and lose your way. Keep going. Just keep your eyes on the object and pretend you are tracing it with your pencil onto the journal page. When you arrive back at your starting point, congratulations! You've done it!

Now, have a look at your sketch. What do you notice about it? How did you feel while you were making it? What went through your mind? Did you resist the whole way, or was there a moment you sank into a meditative state?

• • • • •

Like our other sketching exercises, blind contour drawing is not about making exquisite art or focusing on the end result. It is about the experience—what happens to us when we are moving our hands across the page. Having said that, I do love the energy and interesting elements these drawings possess. They invariably have an edgy, abstract vibe that is compelling.

Rather than a specific artistic outcome, doing these sketches blindly is about letting ourselves get lost on purpose and discovering that that is often the best way to find our way.

Blind contour drawing enables us to travel without leaving our seat. It connects us to the most resonant parts of our intuition and clarity by easing us into letting go. We learn how to quiet our minds. By surrendering into no mind, we can touch the ethereal and the elusive. We can reside in the realm of magic, creation, joy, wonder, and seeing with new eyes. It's all right there, available to us, and we can access it by sketching.

Interestingly, we can ignite this part of our brain anytime we desire. Doing so turns on our creativity for all kinds of other tasks, like brainstorming ideas, thinking up innovative solutions to vexing challenges, approaching problems with fresh eyes, and/or seeing a strategic path for unraveling a business or personal puzzle.

Here is where things get even more interesting. Select a problem or challenge you have been trying to think through or solve. Assign your brain the task of working on it right after you finish your sketch and notice how differently your brain approaches problem solving and idea iteration. Roadblocks in your thinking that you previously grappled with will loosen their grip on you. New ways of framing the issue at hand will come to mind. Pathways to novel solutions will become clear.

My client Claire had a tight deadline for completing a sales page for a new product launch, and she was frustrated with stalled creative flow. She knew the clock was ticking and could not find her way to compelling copy. She texted me in a panic, and I encouraged her to take fifteen minutes to do a blind contour drawing. Claire nearly had a coronary and typed me a text with colorful language in all caps, but to her credit, she did the exercise. Two hours later, she sent me a sheepish apology and an image of a tight first draft.

I use sketching to enter a calm, unfettered state that lets me see the path to ski safely between business challenge moguls. From atop a black diamond run in thick fog, I can squint via sketching. Block out the mental noise and let the best way forward reveal itself to me. I use sketching to connect dots of ideas, create content, negotiate contracts, attract clients, map out priorities, and produce intellectual property. Anything that requires inspired lift, authenticity, vulnerability, fresh perspective, mental clarity, or soothed nerves gets a boost from sketching.

Remember: We can claim our innate creativity at a moment's notice. It is always available. It is simply a matter of shifting into a different processing mode and loosening our imagination and inventiveness by engaging our bodies.

Creating Your Way to Freedom

"but i had something big inside me that i wanted and had to say and if I hadn't written that book, i don't think i would feel free."
AMANDA PALMER

Singer, songwriter, and performance artist Amanda Palmer sat in a bar in Melbourne and wrote the first words of what would become *The Art of Asking: Or, How I Learned to Stop Worrying and Let People Help*. She would go on to write thousands of words a day for two months before beginning the slog phase of editing.

Amanda celebrated her milestone in a Facebook post, which I read with a pounding heart as I took in her words: "if i hadn't written that book, i don't think i would feel free." When something resonates with us on a cellular, knowing level, we shake with adrenaline as the message courses through us.

I put down my phone and picked up my pen and journal. On the back of the page where I had already written notes for goals and desires in progress, I wrote "CREATIVITY & FREEDOM" in all caps. I wanted to capture a hint of what Amanda had revealed in her post so I could return to it later and dig around in her words for clues.

I flipped the page back over. I scanned the notes of my vision for the coming year that I had written several weeks prior. The word "freedom" appeared over and over. I was reminded that when I get right down to it, freedom is what I am after. It not only lies beneath my goals and desires for what I want to create in my work and life, but also forms the core of my "why" in my work with entrepreneurs.

Even though I'm not feeling trapped in my life or business now, I still want to feel more freedom. Not only do I want it for myself, but I am also deeply passionate about helping my clients who are feeling trapped set themselves free.

There are many roads to freedom. We can arrive by creating wealth, flexible schedules, acts of service, and/or beautiful lifestyles and businesses tailored to our unique rhythms, preferences, interests, and skills.

Arriving on wheels powered by our creativity, though, follows a journey of rich self-discovery in reconnecting heart and soul threads that were pulled apart years, decades, ago. Creating something from our depths holds the power to heal us, complete us, and cement soul contracts with others. The stirrings that have been clamoring to shake us, wake us, will not be denied, and will surround us with prison bars if we refuse their bids.

Let's pause and consider what would feel like prison for us if we did not express or create it. Conversely, what feels like our key to freedom, if we created or expressed it?

We already know. We've known all along. We may have been masters of denial as we shelved our dream in the darkness of our Someday Closet. But now, we can choose something else.

We can choose freedom. We can choose to create. We have an idea. A craving to express something. A desire to build and/ or launch the inkling that keeps us awake. A passion to make an indelible impact. We burn to escape the bounds of the mundane. The routine. The infinite gerbil wheel of sameness. We ache for color, play, adventure, traveling to our edges.

Culture tells us we should want all the shiny things, but what we really want more than anything else is to feel alive. And buried deep inside us is the knowledge that the way from "there" to the "here" we crave is through the joyful work and art that ignites us, transforms us. In our becoming, we leave faint trails for others to follow while we change the world as we change ourselves.

Chances are we'll avoid this journey for as long as we possibly can. We often choose to hang back, off to the side, out of frame, and in perceived safety. The longer we ignore the call to step forward into the unknown—toward the blank page, the opportunity, beginning in earnest the vulnerable, real work— the harder it is to make the first mark.

The bridge across the chasm between staying stuck and getting started begins to fade, wear away with each hour. Each day we decide to cling to the painful world we know adds another layer we must ultimately pierce.

The longer we avoid, the harder it is to begin.

"The object of art is not to make salable pictures. It is to save yourself."

Sherwood Anderson

Getting Started
· · · · · · · · · · · · · · · ·

So how do we find our way into the work that we know will
be challenging but rewarding? How can we breathe courage
into the center of our hearts and get to our blank pages, index
cards, and prototypes?

I have made a ritual of sorts for piercing the veil of getting started. I begin by gathering the items I need, like a chef
arranging her mise en place. I leave nothing to chance, knowing that if I have to go in search of a tool, a note, an art supply,
I can deftly use this distraction to avoid the work.

With everything set up properly, I muster my willingness to
make my first mark. This is the moment on which everything
else hinges: reaching forward where nothing currently exists
and placing something onto the blank surface. It seems so simple, innocuous. Yet our minds will want to make this moment
one of life or death—monumental, as if an error or misstep
here is one from which we cannot recover.

It is the only way we ever create anything. That first mark
is the beginning of the conversation, not the end. It is the first
call in what will become a series of calls and responses. We put
down the first mark, the first word, the first line, the first step.
What follows is the reaction to that first effort, formed by our
intuition as to where to take it next.

Artist Ralph Steadman says, "There's no such thing as a
mistake, really. It's just an opportunity to do something else."
He begins his paintings by picking up his pen and making a
strong flip of his wrist, forming a giant ink splat on the white
paper. Steadman studies the ink splat and then decides what
to make of it. The entirety of his artwork is born of those initial marks. Once a mark is on the page, he has something to
fuel his intuition and build upon. And by choosing to "go bold"
with his first mark, he bolsters his creative energy, and the
energy communicated via his work, and swats away self-doubt.

This can be true for all of us. But it's easy to forget. The wolves of self-doubt started circling me during the fifth(!) draft of this book. Gone were my rhythm and carefree approach to creating. My mind had gone uncharacteristically blank. As I cowered in fear, I tried to squint and see their body composition, every hideous hair of their being. Before their fangs could find my jugular and pronounce me creatively dead, I saw it, the source of their power: a dark zone composed of the fear of harsh judgment. The fear of vulnerability, of being fully seen. Exposed and shivering in the limiting belief that my work would not be good enough.

That old fear *again*? Hadn't I soundly healed those ancient wounds long ago? I had forgotten the cardinal rules of creativity that I teach to my coaching clients: 1) evict the squatters of self-doubt and the fear of judgment by keeping the editing and critiquing phase far away from your creating phase, and 2) the process of art-making teaches us how to trust ourselves.

The making and editing states need to remain separate and distinct because the editor in us will crush our initial efforts under a boot of critical disdain, stopping our flow. Let the work and us be open to possibility, to chance. That's where the energy of our creative work connects with us, through us, to those we most want to reach.

To do our best work, we have to be willing each day to climb out onto the skinny branches of vulnerability and uncertainty. The more we tap into what we do not dare bring to the surface for scrutiny (by ourselves or anyone else), the further out we edge onto the thin limbs.

Out on the ends of those tender branches, beyond our second-guessing and fears of failure, the space to flow resides. If we stop and question or doubt, we wobble. If we then indulge in more self-questioning, off our perches we go, falling through the strata of hard-fought progress all the way to the ground.

How can we keep all the aspects of ourselves we appreciate and depend on for our business success while accessing the creative fruit at the ends of those skinny branches? How can we amplify our creative, loose, wild, free selves and bring those parts of us into a symbiotic dance with our striving, strategic selves?

We first must recognize that the two states of being (strategic, careful, calculating, and intellect-driven as opposed to divergent-thinking, free, loose, carefree, wild, and soul-driven) cannot exist simultaneously. We can, though, swing very effectively between them, tagging one for certain tasks and desired outcomes, then switching mindsets and tagging the other for different sensibilities and results.

Liberation in our work (and in our hearts) results from developing both mindsets and becoming nimble in switching between the two. Note that we should be mindful to have ample buffer time between the two states. As we'll see in chapter 5, we don't want to gallop from one to the other and back again without a period of stillness and rest, time to assimilate the lessons of the work.

Here, it becomes even more powerful and potent: if we satisfy our strategic, careful, and intellect-driven self by planning out the rough edges of how we are going to approach a task or create something new, and then tag the other side of us and indulge in dropping fully into a playful approach of creating, we edge right over the flow threshold without stirring our perfect-progress self.

That is, if we choose to start with a bit of structure, we can jettison some, most, or all of it once we get going. During that window of giddy, uncontrolled creating, we stop stressing over perfection and become profoundly present.

We lean more into our intuition as our confidence reserves fill. When we're confident, we can address mistakes, improve, learn, iterate, and course-correct; we make the bold moves our best innovations require.

While over time we develop the sense of when to switch from one mode to the other, know now that we all already have this skill. We are simply supremely skilled in overriding it and ignoring it.

When we turn inward, we can feel the need to have a break from one state of being. We can honor that by stopping ourselves, getting up, and having a break from the work. When we return, we can consciously switch to a different mode of creating. Back and forth, never tiring either set of muscles or draining acuity.

If we resist the urge to look down, and remain squarely seated in our authenticity and our willingness to "go bold" while we create, the realm of flow rewards us with access to our intuition and imagination. We can choose to hold back the lapping waves of the Bay of Others' Opinions and keep them from eroding the shoreline of us. Self-trust serves as our bridge across the chasm of doubt. The wolves retreat, setting us free.

As we bring both sides of ourselves to the vulnerable work we know is our charge, we leave the realm of forced, limited influence and burst into the full capacity of what we can offer, reaching our ideal clients with inspiring impact.

exercise The First Step

In your journal, write the following statement: "If I do not do or create _____ , I do not think I will ever feel free." Now, set a timer and give yourself at least thirty minutes to brainstorm. Underneath the statement, write all of the things that come to mind. Let the page be messy, disjointed. Just focus on getting down everything that pops into your mind.

If it helps to spur your thinking, go back and review your journal. Look at all your notes and scan for themes, connecting threads. What seems to return over and over? What is calling to you to do or create? Get it all down.

Next, take a few minutes to answer this question in your journal: Where am I avoiding making that first mark or move?

Try to identify the first action step that scares you the most. Keep pressing rewind in your mind as you think about doing the work that will set you free. For example, if you want to write a book, is the scariest first action step getting clarity on precisely what the big idea of the book would be? Write that down. If you are considering launching a new enterprise or new product or service, do you fear your idea won't have traction in the market? Or that you don't have enough experience or the right team to pull it off? Or do not know how to find the resources you need? Write that down.

· · · · ·

Regardless of your answers, we can always identify a first step to get started: a phone call, an email, an ask. We give ourselves all of the reasons for not doing the thing that calls to our hearts, but those reasons can almost always be readily debunked. There is a moment we decide to begin, understanding that knowing all the answers and details along the path ahead is not necessary. We are clever, problem-solving beasts, after all. We can figure it out as we move forward.

Piercing the veil between the dreaming and the doing, between sitting on the sidelines and making our first mark, is the real work.

Decide today that you have spent enough time in limbo. You do not need to feel ready, qualified, talented, or able. Simply scoop up the materials you need and flip that wrist. Let the ink fly and land where it chooses.

Study it. Let your intuition take you from there. Each reaction builds upon the one before, ultimately forming the finished work and a life composed of joyful moments, feeling truly alive. Confidence and clues for how to keep going come in the doing. Freedom is right on its heels.

The first step in this process is to observe our inner critic and see that it is just a part of us. Yours is no bigger, hairier, or meaner than anyone else's. Each inner critic is hideous and set upon derailing us from our connection to the rapture of being alive. If we let its negative chatter go unaddressed, we can put our eyes and ears right on it, call it out, and then hush it for long enough to get our hands moving.

The labeling part of our brain is in cahoots with our inner critic. It wants to define what it is we can do, narrowly boxing in and limiting our talent and ability. After observing the troll-speak, our next job is to quiet and disorient the labeling brain, to remove language from the experience.

This is why I argue that we all should stop whatever we are doing right now, tap ourselves on our heads, and declare ourselves artists. Once self-anointed, perhaps we can leap-frog over whether we are "good enough" to make brush strokes or sentences on white surfaces, and simply get going. Because when we create, we are as transformed as the canvas or blank page.

Lynda Barry touches upon this in a conversation with Debbie Millman on the *Design Matters* podcast: "The line itself is giving you an idea ... That drawing can go not just from your head to the page, but definitely from the page and up your hand and into your head."

How much time do we waste fretting over the product instead of considering the transformational power of the process? How often do we euthanize our ideas, passion, and intuition so we never get them down on paper, breathe life into them, or give them a chance to thrive?

Lynda's art teacher at The Evergreen State College gifted her with startling advice. "We were looking at a drawing that I did," Lynda tells Debbie, "and I said, 'I don't really like this drawing. I don't even know how I feel about it. I don't think I like it,' and [my art teacher] paused, and she went, 'It's none of your business.' That was the fulcrum. That's the crucial moment of my entire career."

This advice applies to all of us. Draw, paint, write, collage, sketch. *The result is none of your business.* It's what is happening in the moment of creation that is the point. What is happening inside your body. Your mind. Your soul. Your heart.

What part of you are you transcending? What insights and truths bubble to the surface? What is ignited? What is finally quelled so that you have peace? What is longing to be created in and through you that has nothing to do with what is on the page? What has leapt from your page and traveled up your arm and into your head?

Remember: When we are stuck or in a holding pattern, we will often say to ourselves that we aren't moving because of fear. It's not just fear. It's fear rooted in a lack of self-trust that stops us.

"I'M SO FRUSTRATED!" my prospective client Sarah wailed. "This is taking forever! Am I ever going to get to where I want to be? I've got this huge launch scheduled for the end of this year, and I'm totally procrastinating. I have hardly done any work at all to build out the infrastructure for it. That's not like me! And to top everything off, my weight loss progress has totally stalled out. I just want to be done already and hit my goals! Can you help me?"

After speaking with Sarah for over an hour, it was clear that she was grappling with two main issues:

1 Her marketing coach had recommended that she approach building her platform in a way that felt wholly incongruent to her. Rather than questioning the approach, Sarah had tried to force herself to do the work her coach recommended and was getting nowhere.

2 Sarah was, in fact, making a lot of progress on her weight loss goals and had lost more than forty pounds in a year. Healthy, steady progress. But over the last month or two she hadn't been losing weight at the same pace.

The real culprit in both issues was not Sarah's procrastination or her ability to do the work to achieve any of her goals. It was the icky, sticky goo of self-doubt.

When she even thought about building her social media platforms the way her coach had prescribed, Sarah doubted her ability to lay the groundwork for her launch. Because doing the work felt so out of sync and inauthentic to her, her brain resisted and shut down.

Sarah felt no ease, joy, or flow when she attempted to force herself to move forward. And the few times she actually did appear live on social media, her energy was wonky and nothing she did connected with her desired audience. The previously bubbly, bright, and fun woman had faded, and a stiff cardboard cutout stood in her place.

When self-doubt assailed her, Sarah started to slack off on her healthy habits and rituals. She reverted to eating junk food and staying up later than she had in months. Her once-daily workout got pushed back to once a week. The slow slide down the slippery slope had begun. Self-doubt can erode our footing that fast.

"The object isn't to create art, it's to be in that wonderful state which makes art inevitable."

Robert Henri

exercise What's Blocking You?

When we are stuck like Sarah, our first job is to look for anything that has adhered to us that is *not us*—not in alignment with our true nature. In Sarah's case, it was a course of action steps that did not lean into her natural strengths and, in fact, fought against them.

For you, it may be a loved one's expectations or society's idea of how you should act or be. For others, it could be the prevailing cultural perception of what comprises the ideal business or life.

Being stuck is our first clue that we are carrying something that does not belong to us. As unpleasant as it is, it gives us a wonderful opportunity to scout around like a detective in our business and life and search for clues.

Begin to study the ways you are going about achieving your goals. Ask yourself the following questions:

- Is the transformation I desire truly something I want, or am I trying to create change to please someone else?

- When I think about doing the work required, which aspect of the process feels like being trapped? Which parts, if any, feel like freedom?

- When I engage in doing the work required, what is happening inside my body? Do I feel tightness in my shoulders, neck, and/or chest, or a tinge of nausea? Or do I feel open, light, expansive?

Jot down all your answers in your journal over the course of a week or so. Study your notes and see what they reveal. Refuse to believe that something is wrong with you and begin to believe that something is simply off track with your approach.

Next, think back to all the times you felt at home, profoundly centered and confident when in pursuit of the key to transformation. Where were you? What were you doing? Were you working alone or with others? What routines did you follow? What did you tell yourself? What felt natural, doable?

In other words, what soil were you in? What conditions and mindset were present that enhanced your ability to bloom?

Remember the gorgeous, dainty wild iris that grows along the sides of small creeks on the edges of trails in the Appalachian Mountains. It pushes up through cold, damp soil during the early days of spring and stands in its color among all the brown remnants of winter. It flourishes near water and in full sunlight.

Think of yourself as a wild iris. What soil and growing conditions do you need? What is it you are craving more than anything else? What opens you, the true you, and fills you with happiness? What is it you need to weed out of how you work or how you are chasing transformation?

· · · · ·

Of course, like Sarah, we want to arrive and be done already. Cross the finish line. Move on. Be past it, whatever it is. We no longer want to be where we currently are. And painfully, we are not "there" yet. The transformation process puts us squarely "nowhere." In the space of becoming.

But if we can peel away the expectations of others, find the conditions that best support us, and accept that transformation takes time, we can enjoy the otherworld of becoming.

The wild iris prepares quietly for months before it makes its grand debut. If we stay in the daily wins without hurry, we pull what we want right to us.

Finding Creative Flow and
Your Window of Possibility

. . . .

*"If we all did the things we are really capable of doing,
we would literally astound ourselves."*
THOMAS EDISON

"I think I have the equivalent of writer's block for entrepreneurs," my client Carrie said. "Nothing is coming to me. The ideas I am getting feel tired, overused, common. I know my ideal clients are sick of the endless barrage of crap being thrown at them from online marketers, and I absolutely do not want to add to the heap of unremarkable content out there."

"How would you characterize your energy levels and clarity when you sit down to create?" I asked her.

"Uh, a notch above nonexistent," Carrie replied. "Well, maybe not that bad, but pretty low. I start out having a mix of energy and apprehension. Like, I am feeling fairly good but worried the great ideas won't come. I can get going, but it is really slow going. And then my fears are realized when what I make is just more blah, blah, blah."

"And what time do you usually sit down to do this work?" I asked.

"Maybe ten or so in the morning," Carrie replied.

"What do you generally do first?" I asked.

"You know, the regular morning stuff. Get up at six-thirty or so. Clear my email, check in with my team, coffee and a bagel, read some news. Peek at social. Handle a few client matters. Why?"

"Are you up for trying an experiment?" I asked.

"Sure," Carrie said. "Just nothing too weird, right?"

"It's probably going to feel pretty weird at first," I said. "But you are going to love the results."

You may have already spotted where Carrie is unknowingly poking holes in the bottom of her creative energy bucket: her morning routine. She was getting up relatively late (stay with me) and then proceeding to do an entire series of tasks and activities that numbed, distracted, and depleted her, all the way from checking email to eating a bunch of carbs first thing each day.

Here is the new morning routine I prescribed for Carrie:

1 Get up at 5:00.

2 Drink a tall glass of water before enjoying coffee.

3 Do ten minutes of journaling.

4 Do ten minutes of meditating.

5 Work on her project in a notebook or legal pad from 5:45 until 7:00.

6 Shower, get ready for the day.

7 Eat a veggie and light protein–based breakfast without reading or watching anything.

8 At 8:30, look at her phone and computer for the first time.

After two weeks of her following a new morning schedule, we checked in.

"I really hate getting up at five," Carrie said. "I really hate it. But I'll give you this: so many things have shifted for the better for me already. My brain is different at that hour. The ideas are better, and I'm much clearer. I know the other parts of the routine are important, too, especially staying off my phone and not touching my computer until after my creative work is done. It's like I'm fully settled into myself after having been away from who I truly am for ages. It's hard to explain."

"I know exactly what you mean," I said. "I'm thrilled these few changes are working on you as I'd expected. Are you ready to dial it up even more?"

"Oh, no. You mean get up even earlier?"

"Let's just try something and see what happens," I said.

Carrie was a great sport and did experiment with getting up even earlier. She agreed to wake up at 4:30 for one week and then at (gasp!) 4:00 the following week. She found that when she got up at 4:30, she was able to access a new part of her creativity that had previously seemed to be locked away, hidden from her. She more easily slid into a state of flow and ease while working on paper and playing around with mind mapping, blocking out ad copy, writing content, and creating sales funnels.

When she pushed herself further and rose at four in the morning, she didn't find her results were any better or different. Getting up that early simply made her cranky and exhausted. When we shifted to experimenting with waking later and beginning her creative routine later in the day, her results fell off a cliff. Carrie was, much to her dismay, a morning creator.

Carrie's optimal Creative Circadian Rhythm (CCR) turned out to be a window between 4:30 a.m. and 9:00 a.m. After a few months of practice and the positive reinforcement of the incredible results she was enjoying, she was able to incorporate her new CCR into each workday about 80 percent of the time—a solid performance.

"I just feel better," Carrie said six months into her new routine. "I love this new brain of mine. And I'll say this—we are knocking 'em dead out there with the new program we launched. The best signup rate we've ever had, and everyone is loving the content and community. When I learned how to connect with myself at a deep level, I got so much better at connecting with our people."

Are you struggling to access your window of possibility, your deep connection to your creativity? If so, see if you can run a few experiments to determine when your optimal Creative Circadian Rhythm is. Remember, just because Carrie's was early in the morning *does not* mean that yours is too. You might find that a much later window of time is when you hit your stride.

I'm a very different person and writer at 4:00 a.m. than I am at 1:30 p.m. Oddly, it feels as if I'm not even the same person when I attempt creative work outside of my magic hours. When I am in my zone before dawn, I can access a part of my creative brain that is not online to that degree at any other time during the day.

Further, my discipline to do deep and challenging work wanes as the day progresses. I begin each early morning with a topped-off tank of willingness, courage, and determination that propels me forward through times of uncertainty.

If we are willing to tolerate some initial discomfort in finding out where that zone of optimal creating is for us, we can ride the ethereal edges of access to a different world and enjoy a profoundly joyful state of flow.

Don't Make Your Tools Precious

"This business of becoming conscious . . . is ultimately about asking yourself . . . How alive am I willing to be?"
ANNE LAMOTT

Emily Dickinson was very particular about her creativity tools. Her utensils of choice were a stubby pencil and the backs of used envelopes, torn open into sheet-like shapes. I believe she intuited that the more exquisite her paper and writing implements were, the more she'd resist writing. This way, I imagine she could sneak up on her work and get lines down, without waking her inner censor. Once her creativity pump was primed with the production of her first lines, she could find her flow and complete poem after poem.

Understanding such a method gives us insight into how to get those crucial first lines down. The first marks. How to successfully preempt the wrestling and thrashing about with one's muse. Vital guidance for championing what bestselling author Steven Pressfield calls one's Resistance.

Our tendency, though, is to elevate our cherished creativity tools and methods of creating to what Pressfield describes as "precious" status. Don't we often purchase the gorgeous leather journal with gilded pages, the expensive canvas, or the handcrafted fountain pen thinking that each will transport us right over the top of the Resistance hedge and deliver us to creativity nirvana? And don't we often, way too often, let those treasured tools gather dust in the corner, unused, because we fear "messing them up"?

If you were to look at the desk where I am currently sitting, you would spy no fewer than four expertly crafted leather journal covers filled with notebooks with sumptuous Japanese paper. You'd see a cup filled with brush markers, fountain pens, and Blackwing pencils. You'd spot a planner with an abstract art cover, as well as a dozen bright floral notebooks. And on the table next to the window, you'd see bottles and tubes of paint, brushes, sketchbooks, collage papers, pastels, crayons, charcoal, and bags of washi tape, stamps, and stickers. In other words, you'd recognize I have a thing for creativity supplies.

I used to be a collector and never an implementer. Collecting all the gear and cool tools made me feel like I was actually a writer, an artist. I could delude myself for an hour or so during the purchasing process, aligning myself with working artists who actually use their tools.

I want to be clear: If you love the gear and creativity toys as much as I do, by all means, indulge! Collect! Display them proudly. Admire their beauty and enjoy the exhilarating lift of their potential.

But then take a breath, sit down, and use them up. Get them dirty, scratched, marked up. Wear down the nibs and sharpened points. Fill the pages. Rip edges. Coat canvases and paint right over your old work. Paste things into your journal. Free your markers from their cases and zippered pouches.

If you find that you hesitate each time you reach for one of your beloved tools, think about how you might get yourself started with some less-than-precious devices. Stuck outlining a chapter? How about taking a Sharpie to the back of a used paper grocery bag? Not sure how to map out the customer journey on your website? Stand at your easel and clip a piece of newsprint to it. Take a crayon and map out your storyboards. Can't see the strategic plan for next quarter? Get five or six stacks of different colored Post-it notes and start scribbling down all the things you want to have happen. Then start sticking the notes down in the order and flow that works best for you. Rearrange. Crumple and toss the crummy ideas. Revise.

Regardless of the creative task, make it really easy to start and start over. Grab a stubby pencil and get going.

Tools, Architects, and Gardeners
. . . .

"There are two types of writers, the architects and the gardeners. The architects have the whole thing designed and blueprinted out before they even nail the first board up. The gardeners dig a hole, drop in a seed and water it."
GEORGE R.R. MARTIN

In an expansive, lodge-like auditorium nestled among ancient, towering redwoods on the 1440 Multiversity campus, a line formed at the microphone. Internationally renowned authors

Liz Gilbert and Cheryl Strayed sat on the stage ready to field questions from writers and creative entrepreneurs.

Hundreds of us sat, journals open on laps, with our pens poised and ready to take down every morsel of advice the writing giants had to offer.

Predictably, the first question pertained to how they work. A young woman asked Liz and Cheryl what their thought process is. She wanted to know about their respective planning and outline process, if they had one, and how they got started and kept up their momentum.

Liz answered first. She noted her process is always well thought out in advance. She begins with copious research and note-taking. She knows exactly where the book is going at the onset of the project, and by the time the research and note phase is complete, she is ready to sit down and write.

It sounded as if her books just write themselves. She argued for such a process as hers by suggesting that one would never paint a room without a plan, for example, as you could end up with a disaster.

I immediately judged my own creative process very harshly. It didn't remotely resemble hers in the least.

Cheryl sat forward in her chair, smiled, and leaned toward her mic.

She told a different story. In fact, her process is the polar opposite! She simply starts and lets her creativity run wild.

The room exhaled and laughed in relief.

George R.R. Martin, author of the Song of Ice and Fire series (adapted into the Emmy Award–winning TV series *Game of Thrones*), would call Liz an architect and Cheryl a gardener.

Liz builds a solid structure from the ground up, knowing in detail the bones comprising the final project. Cheryl plants idea seedlings, stands back and observes how (and if) they grow, and takes direction for her garden from the organic impulses held within the casings of each kernel.

Two very accomplished writers with two very different creative processes. Neither is better than the other. These creative powerhouses simply have unique personalities and styles.

We live in an architect-favoring culture, one that tells us to have our ducks in a row before we start, our detailed plans and visions well in place. This approach works incredibly well for some of us, but alienates and discourages those with a more spontaneous, follow-the-work-as-it-goes style.

It is important to know which approach suits our inherent style. Once we know if we are more of an architect or a gardener, we can champion our comfort with, and confidence in, our creativity. Sometimes we may need to be an architect or a gardener for certain phases of the project. For example, I was a gardener for several years when I began writing this book. I went to the farmer's market of ideas, on a quest to figure out how inspiration and creativity were linked. I filled my basket with inklings, research questions, and hypotheses. I planted, cultivated, tended, and harvested for months. Got my first draft down. Then switched over to architect mode for structure, clarity, organization, and editing when writing subsequent drafts.

Ask yourself: What approach best suits this part of my project right now? Or, if you are stuck, try switching modes to see if you can dislodge something and find flow.

Delving into any creative project tests us, rattles us. It is tempting to look around and seek direction from others as to which way of working is "right."

If a gardener believes the creative lore, she may wait and wait to have a perfect plan in place before she starts. As a result, she might never write that book, paint that painting, take that culinary class, or launch that business!

I believe we hunger to hear of other creatives' processes and rituals because we haven't fully explored our own, or haven't yet embraced our personal style. We may even think there is something inherently wrong with how we work and create.

Or maybe, if we are really honest with ourselves, we haven't actually done the work to truly know what our rhythms and routines are.

Regardless, we'd all do well to heed the call to action worded by Irish poet John Anster: "What you can do or dream you can, begin it. Boldness has genius, power and magic in it. Begin it now."

Beginning may look like gathering and mapping out neat piles of note cards with plans, or it may look like working with only a whisper of an idea and winging it.

Whichever approach you choose to embrace, have the assurance it is right, as it is yours. You might have to swat away the dark dog sitting on the edge of your desk, snarling and growling that you have no business whatsoever tackling this project, this dream.

Take your seat anyway.

Our words, paint strokes, ingredients, or business strategies will come. Our ideas will drop into us and form, leading us like stepping stones in a garden. Our vision and message will rise in us, taking us to heights and lines of sight we never dreamed we could reach, breaking the bonds of our earthly concerns.

exercise What Creativity Tools Do You Have?

Let's try on all kinds of creativity tools and approaches to doing our work. Take an inventory of the tools you have on hand. Gather them all together in one spot and write down everything you have in your journal.

Decide what you'd like to bring out of retired status and into active duty. What are you making precious? Select several things that you've always loved but were afraid to use. If you don't have a collection of tools, go on a fun trip to an art or stationery store and select a few things that call to you. What looks fun? Playful? Which designs light you up?

Begin to track which materials you gravitate to. What works for you? What feels stiff or too scary to use? Write down all your findings in your journal.

Next, let's track your winning creativity processes and Creative Circadian Rhythm of making something. When do you have the most energy? The most clarity? When do you have some kind of ethereal access to flow, ideas, willingness to be bold? What are you doing? At what time of day? How are you approaching the work? What were you doing right before you did the work? Are you more of an architect or gardener? Do you switch back and forth between the two approaches? Take a page from author and researcher Jim Collins and study yourself like a researcher would study a bug. What makes the bug (you) happy and confident? What makes the bug do the work? Get it all down in your journal.

· · · · ·

We all want to know the right tools or precise artistic process that will float us over the top of any and all challenges. That is a false search. That is the job of doing the work. It is perfectly fine and helpful to learn about how others work so that we may "try on" different tools, methods, and processes. Know, though, that the job of finding the tools and processes best suited to us is up to us alone. And the only way to find our fit is to jump in there and experiment. Please remember not to make your discoveries mean anything. They just are. If we do not have the same habits, tools, or ways of working as our heroines or heroes, no matter. Do not try to force a way of working onto yourself. We come alive when we find our fit, our rhythm. It may take a while. Patience is key. Keep going.

Becoming an Insider to Your Creativity

....

"If you've ever had that feeling of loneliness,
of being an outsider, it never quite leaves you."
TIM BURTON

I grew up in Highlands, a gorgeous small town perched on a plateau at an elevation of 4,118 feet. A community that boasted three traffic lights (we would later add one more) and a year-round population of 2,500 people. At the time, most of the inhabitants were "locals"—direct descendants of original settlers with family ties going back multiple generations.

My mom and dad were from Dayton, Ohio, and Miami, Florida, respectively, and moved to Highlands in 1959. So while I was born at an area hospital and lived in Highlands for the first seventeen years of my life, I was never really considered "local."

I skipped the second grade and entered into a new culture at age seven, with classmates nearly two years older. It took me a few weeks to acclimate to the schoolwork, and while I really loved my new classmates, I did not feel at home in the wooden desk in the middle of the third row.

Although I wouldn't come to identify the feeling until many years later, the combination of not being local and being a younger newcomer to the class placed me on the outside like an electron, ever orbiting the nucleus of the unreachable inner circle.

Combined with my painful shyness, being an outsider served as a filter that kept me from joining in with cliques and established insiders. By high school, I was most definitely part of the "in" crowd, yet, as Tim Burton attests in the quote above, I never lost that destabilizing sense of not quite being in step with the music of others.

Decades later, when my marriage fell apart and we lost our home, the feelings of exile returned like a winter season that wouldn't relent to spring. I began to wonder where I did feel at home, and even what "home" was.

Was home a static place, composed of wood, glass, and walls with a front door and a driveway? Was home the community in which you lived? Or was it where you grew up? Or the place with which you most identified?

I decided to define home as a state of being. Home, to me, is creating. The feeling I get when writing, making something. It is the connection to myself, to what I'm thinking, to what I didn't even know I thought or felt before moving my hands to write, to create. It is a lightness of being that burbles and floats upward inside my veins and organs, taking my spirit along with it. It is being seated inside myself and my own voice, knowing what my truth is, and having the courage to give it form and release it into the wild.

When I am cut off from my creativity, anxiety builds and builds. The distance between the homeland of my true self and the self I present to the world grows. Pressure mounts within me. Like a newly arrived immigrant, I stand on the shore of myself and look across the water, back toward my homeland, feeling the depths of exile.

We often incorrectly expect the world of creativity to be closed. Closed to us. It is we, though, who are often closed to ourselves. Sealed off from our purpose. When we are cut off from our creativity, the pain we experience is the loss of connection to ourselves. We are exiled, unmoored, lost.

The world of creativity, though, is open, as open as we'll let ourselves be. And it is filled with surprises, connections, purpose, light, guidance, fulfillment, joy—*buoyancy*.

When we get going and finally return to creating, something else joins in with us, helps us keep going and cross the

"The moment you've uttered the exact dimensionality of your exile, you're already turning towards home."

David Whyte

finish line. That something comprises our intuition and willingness to follow its tiny threads. It is powered by divinity, grace, and alignment.

Our brain wants to control how things unfold. There's nothing but dead air there. The way home is mapped by detaching from outcomes and filling our lungs with playfulness. Turning away from expectations.

exercise Where Are You Not at Home?

Let's get clear on all the ways we are in exile. What does not fit for us right now? What are we doing that alienates us from our true selves? Take twenty minutes right now and write down in your journal all the ways you are not at home within yourself. Set a timer.

When the time is up, review what you have written with a profoundly compassionate heart. Breathe in deeply what has felt like an odd disconnection from the world, from your essential nature.

Turn now, gently, toward whatever you think of as home. The place of resonance, balance, and freedom that unifies your disparate fragments and seats you back into your cells, skin, bones, and unique energy.

We are in good company in our loneliness, our exile. Each of us is aware of the sting of being an outsider and each of us is desperate to find belonging. When we connect our unique truth, vision, and voice to our hands and create with courage, we simultaneously build and inhabit a space and time that is hearth and home.

* * * * *

"Things right now feel like one giant test after another," my client Ron said. "I can barely stay focused for ten minutes at a time. I'm trying to hold together an international virtual team, and I can sense my key leaders are drained, losing focus and energy. I'm worried about my family and how we are all going to handle this move across six states. I thought a fresh start would do us all good, but now it feels like I'm just trying to outrun my problems."

Ron paused, and I waited in silence.

He exhaled loudly and said, "Maybe the thing that scares me the most right now is that I don't think I've got what it takes. This feeling of being truly lost, and, for the first time in my life, I cannot see the way out."

Ron had named it. The thought beneath what was driving how he felt and, consequently, his actions and results: "I don't think I've got what it takes."

Each time I begin to work on a sizeable creative project, try something I've never done before, or push myself outside of my comfort zone into new entrepreneurial territory, that zinger of a crappy thought pops right out of my brain and sends me spinning.

If I let that thought float around inside my head unaddressed, it glues me into place, afraid to make a decision or get going.

Recently, when that thought came calling, I went to the woods and tried to hike the creative paralysis out of my body and mind. After an hour or so of being immersed in towering trees and quiet, it occurred to me that I could create a preemptive thought, a personal philosophy, that might defang the thought dragon before it could land a blow to my confidence.

I asked myself what it is I believe when I am at my best, and how I could combine that belief with qualities I admire most in others. Taking inspiration from Eleanor Roosevelt and Hermann Hesse, I stood in the middle of the trail and wrote the following in my journal: "My personal philosophy: I do the things I think I cannot do and live in accordance with my true self."

The moment I had it down, I knew its power. The words rang true for me and reminded me of who I truly am. Of course, we all have moments of doubt, of veering off course, of floundering. But what separates those who push through to the other side and those who stay stuck is a battle of thoughts and beliefs.

exercise What to Do When You Are Lost

What are you working on right now that feels too hard? Where are you lost? See if you can craft your own personal philosophy to pry yourself loose and into action, now and in the future. Ask yourself a series of questions and write your answers in your journal:

- When I'm at my best, what beliefs lie just beneath the surface of my thoughts and actions? That is, when I'm rocking it, what is it I think is true? What do I believe I am capable of doing?

- Who do I know who demonstrates characteristics and qualities I greatly admire?

- What are those qualities?

- What are my favorite quotes? My favorite words?

Once you've answered these questions, circle the words that stand out to you and cross out the ones that don't. After studying what's left, try to come up with a phrase or sentence that lines up with who you are and how you want to live your life.

Share the draft with a loved one, ask for input, and fine-tune your philosophy from there. Then commit it to memory and recite it daily.

When you find yourself in quicksand, hesitant to begin work on a project or lost in the weeds during one underway, return to your personal philosophy and say aloud, "I'm the kind of person who _____ [add in your personal philosophy here]."

Remind yourself that being lost is temporary; it is a place to refuel and recalibrate. It is not an indicator of your ability, talent, or worth. It is just a moment in time. A place of in between. A much-needed pause to refresh your energy and gather up what you need for the rest of the journey.

4

Putting Your True Self Back at the Helm

"I am not who I think I am.
I am not who you think I am.
I am who I think you think I am."

CHARLES COOLEY.

WHEN WE refuse to be concerned about what others think about us or our work, we start to find our way to back to our true nature and bring our creativity back online. This requires courage and an awareness of all of the outside influences that have blurred and erased the edges that define us. Little by little, we pick up clues, dissolve others' expectations, and become ourselves once more. We redraw who we truly are and risk showing the tender image against scrutiny.

As we reveal our true selves, we send out signals that stir the consciousness of the collective—most notably, our ideal clients. We may even inspire and awaken those who have also been asleep at the wheels of their own lives and help them heal their hearts as we heal our own.

By igniting our inner rebel, we remember that the people, places, and things we love are ours and ours alone to love. They offer clues to how we may connect to what calls to us most deeply.

When we stand in our integrity and are mindful truthtellers, our voices are clear, traveling across time and distance. We pull our desired futures and markets toward us as we forge bonds, link by link, daisy-chaining a circle of authentic community around us.

I LOOKED at Adam across the patio table and marveled at how grown up he was, how tall he was, not just in stature but also in character. I was on fire with motherly pride and love.

"Well, of course, you are welcome to stay with me while you figure things out and decide upon your next move," I said.

His face brightened and then a deep awareness fell like a curtain.

"Thank you so much. I love being with you, but I'm afraid you'll turn my neck," he said.

I howled, laughing. "What do you mean?"

"I'm not sure," he said, searching his enormous feet for answers.

I sat up straight and leaned toward him. "What you just said feels very profound. It feels important that we both understand what you mean. Let's try to unpack it."

We chatted for a while, kicking around theories and ideas. And then we landed right on it. What my son meant was that he needed to be alone in order to hear, see, think, and feel for himself who *he* believes he is. He needed to dissolve all expectations from me, and everyone, to keep his focus where it should be—on listening to the voice inside him. The voice of his true self.

"I'd say you are well on your way, honey. Stay with it. Keep going. And don't ever lose your uncanny ability to stay in alignment with what your heart is asking from you."

I replayed this conversation over and over in my mind and intuited there was more for me to understand and learn from it. Every time I heard my son's words land, I felt a jolt from head to stomach, urging me to dig deeper.

When I stopped forcing, the insight showed up. I was up to my elbows in suds, washing a giant soup pot, when I heard my own voice inside my head say: *Our Art against Artifice.*

My mind became a screen, flashing images of notes from research I have been doing for the last several years. Note cards, journal pages, sticky notes, articles highlighted in orange ink, and waterproof sheets scribbled upon in the shower flashed in my mind's eye.

I leaned into the soup pot, propped my forearms on the edge of the sink, lowered my head, and closed my eyes. I realize now that I was trying to listen as I've never listened before.

Halfway into the kitchen sink, I began connecting my conversation with my son to everything I have been reading, learning, and writing about for years—the essence of the Creative Rebel's Voyage.

This book's elusive through line made itself visible and motioned to me to come closer. I shook the suds from my hands and wrists and dashed to my laptop to write.

DAVID WHYTE'S poetry describes what he refers to as the conversational nature of reality, the notion that there is an ongoing meeting between the edges of who we are and the periphery of others' expectations. At that frontier, we seek to distinguish what is us from everyone else's influence upon us. As we listen in quiet solitude to our own knowing and truth, the push from others, whether overt or covert, begins to dissolve.

Solitude is key to surfacing our true selves. We need solitude to reclaim our authentic nature, as it is in the stillness of quiet that our desires, dreams, insights, and intuition dare to lift their chins to speak to us.

In the film *Adaptation*, written by Charlie Kaufman, Charlie and his twin brother, Donald, have a revealing conversation while hiding in a swamp. Charlie shares a memory of high school, when he watched his brother talk and flirt with the girl Donald was in love with. She was sweet to him to his face, but when Donald walked away, she started making fun of him with one of her friends. Charlie discovers that Donald had heard her and struggles to understand how his brother had remained happy and still loved her. Donald tells him that your love is your own, and no one can take it from you: you are who you love, not the other way around. Charlie, who always worries about what others think of him, feels freed from the burden of others' expectations and opinions, and realizes that these things are *none of his business.*

You are who you love, not who loves you. It's in the adoption of "it's none of my business what other people think" where we all find sovereignty. It's there that you discover how to be true to yourself and walk through the door free of the crippling judgment we and others place on ourselves. We open way up because no harm can come to us when we do. We can show it all, be it all, give it all. This is the moment, far from shore, that our sails fill with wind on our Creative Rebel's Voyage.

It is here that we begin our journey of remembering and becoming our true selves. And as we share what we are learning about ourselves through our work and creative expression, the art of us in all forms, we not only learn more about what is us and what is periphery but also help others find their way.

As we find our courage, we help others find their courage. We find our art, what it is we want to say and be and do most of all, through the courage to make bad art, through the willingness to not know what we are doing. Through honesty. Through getting it wildly "wrong." As Kaufman notes, in this tolerance of being fully seated in uncertainty, more of who we truly are can take shape—and provide inspiration to others seeking the same:

> Say who you are, really say it in your life and in your work. Tell someone out there who is lost, someone not yet born, someone who won't be born for 500 years ... [I]f you are honest about who you are, you'll help that person be less lonely in their world because that person will recognize him or herself in you.

We are not the elaborate artifices we construct. Those are simply built-in responses to what we've been taught and told. We lay the bricks that form the wall of our fortress against exposure, scrutiny, and judgment. But we wield that wall against ourselves too. When we're behind those bricks, others can't truly know us, and, painfully, we can't truly know ourselves either.

And in that place of subterfuge and false constructs of self, we are lonely. No one can see or hear us. We are ever fearful of being found out. The irony is that being found out is our key to freedom and creative fire. The key to our precious, unique voice and way of seeing and being in the world.

To atomize and dissolve this self-imposed exile, we must first acknowledge its presence and hold on us. Then we can begin to listen. What feels like truth? What feels like freedom? What feels like vise grips on our limbs and heart?

What can we pull up from the mud and onto the potter's wheel of us into a shape that feels like home and our true nature? That gloppy, shapeless mess is as beautiful and breathtaking as the final, fired vessel.

It is us: Our Art against Artifice.

Archaeology of the Self: Digging for Your Authentic Nature

"Indeed, the Artist is no other than he who unlearns what he has learned, in order to know himself."
E.E. CUMMINGS

On a sunny Saturday in 2005, I nearly sprinted from the parking lot to the classroom where my Innovation and Creativity class would be starting soon. I was eager to see my fellow students in the Master of Entrepreneurship program and soak up the brilliance of my professors. Being back in school invigorated and opened me. I had been working as a real estate broker for four years, and while I was very successful, my brain wanted stimulation, to be stretched and pulled, pushed to its limits.

We sat in a large "U" facing a screen in front of the blackboards. After a brief introduction to the video we were about to see, one of my professors switched off the lights. The moment the room went dark marked the end of one version of me.

The ABC News *Nightline* episode with Ted Koppel began with a series of black-and-white images portraying straitlaced employees performing hyper-organized work in corporate offices. In places like these, people always defer to the boss. But, asked the voice of David Kelley, founder of Palo Alto design firm IDEO, was the boss always going to have the best ideas? Not likely.

Then the camera cut to an employee shooting a ball through a toy hoop in the fun and colorful IDEO office space. With a smile, Kelley introduced the space as "where the crazies lived," and, importantly, where they did their work.

Watching, I wriggled in my seat and felt my heart flutter. I smelled and felt the electricity in the air and knew something was about to happen, the way you can tell a summer storm is upon you before you see or hear it.

For a little under half an hour, the episode featured the IDEO design-thinking process as they redesigned an ordinary shopping cart, revealing a highly creative organization and culture:

- No idea was judged or deemed bad; instead, they encouraged "wild ideas."

- Everyone had the freedom to express themselves fully.

- There was a joyfulness, a playfulness in working in a diverse community of "T-shaped" people (those with broad backgrounds as well as deep knowledge in a particular field).

- They took an anthropological, ethnographic approach to market research, and infused it into their design-thinking process.

I felt as if I were dreaming with my eyes open as I watched. Then one of the design leads in the video said: "Enlightened trial and error succeeds over the planning of the lone genius."

The top of my head came off.

Concrete, formed around the soul of me, my authentic self, over the course of thirty-nine years, cracked in racing fissures. Chunks of limiting beliefs, small and fearful thinking, accumulated during a lifetime of listening to how others thought I should live, calved from my core and hit the floor.

His comment perfectly captured what excited me about how IDEO worked and created. You don't have work under the knives of judgment. You don't have to go it alone. You can experiment and play in a group of innovative, fun people and solve things together. The way to creativity is to be wild, bold. Unapologetically yourself. Your voice and vision matter. You can positively impact the world, one idea, one person at a time.

IDEO was like the company version of my dad, championing possibility thinking, tuned always to the needs of customers. David Kelley also shared many things in common with Dad: warmth, kindness, and gentleness in an engineer-artist-entrepreneur body. IDEO brought me home to myself and reminded me of what I knew to be true.

That moment marked the beginning of my new life. The moment I was inspired to learn absolutely everything I could about innovation and creativity. I began doing deep research and prototyped an initial methodology for working with entrepreneurs, corporate teams, and nonprofit leaders. In 2006, I launched the first version of the Innovation & Creativity Institute (ICI) and built the company while I slowly scaled back my real estate work. I continued to do research and work with clients, folding new revelations from both into my methodology and fine-tuning my approach, curriculum, and tools. My young company garnered traction and early wins.

Two years later, in the fall of 2008, my life imploded. The financial markets crashed, cratering my family's financial well-being and delivering what would be a death blow to my marriage.

I was in shock, stunned by fear and sadness. I kept trying to restart my brain, desperate to find some path out. I called a divorce attorney and asked him how I should approach solving the mess we were in. Surely there was a strategy he could recommend. His reply was swift and firm: "Susie, you are in a boat in the middle of the ocean, and it's taking on water. You need to jump out and start swimming for shore."

In other words, take action. Quit ruminating. Get moving. His words lit a fire under me and gave me the courage to start problem solving.

I immediately set about righting my financial ship. Even though we were in the middle of the Great Recession, I knew I could leverage my years of experience in real estate and was willing to take a giant, risky step. At the beginning of 2011, I launched White Oak Realty Group. In the fall of that year, my husband and I lost our home in foreclosure, and one year later, our divorce was finalized. Even with these devastating setbacks, I had evidence my real estate firm would be a smashing success, so I put my head down and worked with unwavering focus and zeal.

By early 2014, I had paid off all my debt and was financially secure. That very same spring, I renewed my commitment to optimal health and began a circuitous journey to losing weight, establishing healthy habits and rituals, and reclaiming joy. A few months later, I took a solo trip to Paris that set me on a Creative Rebel's Voyage, altering the trajectory of my life once more and connecting me with the passion for creating a buoyant approach to entrepreneurship and my entire life.

I strolled the streets, took in the unending beauty of the city, got my hair and makeup done by world-famous beauticians, hung out at the fashion venues to see the latest street styles, shopped in designer stores, ate the most incredible food, immersed myself in art, and reconnected to a part of myself that I had somehow buried for almost a quarter of a century.

I remembered what I had shelved when life just got busy. I remembered what I truly loved, and decided I was no longer willing to live a life that did not 100 percent reflect my passion, interests, and desires. I was going to live a life of and on purpose.

I remembered that travel has a way of getting under your skin in the best way possible. It provides unending inspiration, adventure, and the ability to see everything with new eyes. It is one of the most powerful conduits to inspired creativity.

In 2015, I began taking sketching, painting, and mixed media art classes. Little by little, I learned how to see, recover my creativity, and finally disbelieve the lie that I was not an artist. As I developed my skills, I changed the ICI curriculum once more, reflecting the lessons in art-making that I was experiencing. With every new creativity course I take, whether in abstract painting or French cooking, I take each insight and enhance and expand how I think, coach, teach, and experience the world. An ever-evolving, delicious process of becoming that benefits my clients and readers.

In 2018, I sold White Oak Realty Group so that I could devote more time to my work with ICI's clients, further develop and hone my creativity, experience more Creative Rebel's Voyages, and write this book.

Profoundly joyful and painful life events had taken a chisel to the concrete obscuring my Golden Buddha, helped me see the lies I was telling myself, the desperate bids to be accepted by those who could not see me. Woke me up to my destiny and delivered spoonfuls of courage to begin living it. On illuminated paths of what could be as well as in dark and lonely corners, I found boldness. Found what I am capable of. What I want to create. How I want to live and work.

In the years since I watched the IDEO *Nightline* episode, I have witnessed hundreds of clients unearth, remember, and reconnect with their passion, desires, and curiosity. Embrace the things that send shock waves of excitement through their bodies as they shake off the habits, beliefs, and expectations that have hidden them from what they truly want, what lights their souls on fire.

Let's chisel concrete. Let's dig for our authentic selves.

exercise Making a Mind Map of Your Ideal Self

Let's go on an archaeological dig to excavate aspects of your true self that may be buried beneath years of sediment, accumulated under the weight of the well-meaning other. We are going to do a mind map. Get a pen and your journal and turn it to a landscape orientation. Write the following words in the middle of the page:

Who would I be and what would I do if I could be anyone and do anything I want?

Draw a circle around those words. Next, begin brainstorming your answers. Place your answers around the page in their own bubbles and connect the bubbles with lines to the center circle. Try to resist the urge to censor yourself or refuse to write something because it doesn't seem realistic or possible. Just get it all down.

You might also glean insight by answering these questions:

- When you see or hear something you believe to be unjust, immoral, or unkind, do you always state your beliefs and/ or act?

- When a friend or loved one asks your opinion on something, do you consistently tell the truth?

- When you are invited or asked to do something you do not want to do, do you easily and simply say no, or do you fabricate an excuse?

- Is the work you are doing right now fulfilling, stretching you in exciting ways, and offering you opportunities to learn, grow, and have an impact?

- Are you in any relationships that drain you or make you unhappy?

What do you see? Notice recurring themes and patterns. Do you have some puzzle pieces, some early clues? Don't try to force answers or insight; just explore. Flip the paper over and take five minutes to journal about what came up for you. When you are finished writing, put your journal aside and let your subconscious mind continue to work on it for you.

The Tyranny of Perfectionism

*"Nothing can be beautiful that does not take
a calculated risk with ugliness."*
ALAIN DE BOTTON

"I can't do it," my client Thomas said. "I mean, I literally cannot even get started. The man who routinely cranks out all kinds of other work is now completely blank, empty, done."

"What do you think is different this time?" I asked. "Why do you think you are stuck now compared to all of the other times you've been up to bat?"

Thomas was silent for a moment. I stared at my phone and waited.

"The stakes," he said. "This is a huge investor pitch for my company. We need this deal to go through, or we might not be around in six months, you know? Everything about this presentation has to be perfect."

"That was the word I was waiting for," I said.

"What? Which word?" Thomas asked.

"Perfect," I said. "Striving for perfection is the worst briar patch, the most gnarly, tangled mess of lies and painful thoughts. A sure killer of your creativity and, perhaps even more importantly, of your willingness to try new ideas."

"Okay, so what do I do?" Thomas asked. "How do I free myself from the briar patch?"

"Paper," I said. "Lots and lots of paper. And one marker. I'm setting a timer. I'd like you to generate as many shitty ideas as you possibly can in fifteen minutes. All we are after here is volume. Just get ideas down. The shittier, the better."

"Wait," Thomas said. "What's the catch? The goal is idea quantity only?"

"Quantity only. Completely forget quality. In fact, try to push quality away right now."

"I'll admit to being totally confused," Thomas said. "But I'll try it."

"Great! I'll call you back in fifteen minutes on the dot."

When I called Thomas back, his mood had brightened considerably.

"You ought to see this mess," he laughed. "I'm surrounded by piles of paper filled with shitty ideas. You'd be proud of how awful these are."

"Excellent. Dig through the pile now and pick out your favorite one. Read it to me."

I could hear him shuffling through the pages.

"Hmm," Thomas said. "You know, I've got something here that is completely ridiculous, but it could be changed. Worked on. I think I might be able to make something out of it. I wrote down that I should do the presentation dressed as a clown to lighten the mood. But what just occurred to me is that I could wear a costume of sorts. Not a clown costume, of course, but maybe dress up like one of our ideal clients. Or, if not that, start the presentation from their voice. Or maybe tell a story. Oh, that's it. I can start with a very compelling story that really highlights how vital our work is, how transformational it is."

Thomas was on an idea roll. In fifteen minutes, he had pierced through the sticky membrane of perfectionism and had his creative footing back again. By employing a tactic inspired by bestselling author Anne Lamott in her book *Bird by Bird: Some Instructions on Writing and Life*, Thomas was able to generate multiple ideas quickly that eventually led him to an idea he could refine and use.

Lamott cautions us: "Perfectionism is the voice of the oppressor, the enemy of the people. It will keep you cramped and insane your whole life, and it is the main obstacle between you and a shitty first draft." Lamott suggests that we just get something, anything, down. We can then go back and see what we have. Pan for gems. Pluck out the good bits and then rework what was once a shitty draft into new and better drafts.

Perfectionism keeps us jailed in a never-ending loop of "not good enough."

The work is not good enough.

The idea is not good enough.

We're not good enough.

The more times the "not good enough" wheel turns within us, the deeper the tracks become. And the harder they are to escape.

I grapple with the tyranny of perfectionism all the time, most especially when I'm trying something new and, like Thomas, when the stakes are high. I can flounder for hours or even days before I remember my job is first only about quantity, not quality.

And then there is what television and radio personality Ira Glass describes as the painful gap between knowing what great work is and not being skilled enough yet to create to that standard. As Glass points out, it takes a tremendous volume of work to get better, to rise to your own exquisite taste.

If we stand at the gate of our tender, vulnerable souls armed with the simple idea of volume, we can hold the advancing perfectionism soldiers at bay. To get to our great work, we have to embrace our worst work. Let the marks strike the blank page or canvas, marring its pristine surface with smudges, ink, pencil, paint, poor choices. Choices that can be made into better ideas, better work. Work that elevates, that is clear and connects.

Igniting Your Inner Rebel
. . . .

*"Where did I find the courage to rebel, change my life,
live alone? I don't want to over-estimate all this,
but damn it, I love that nine-year-old, whoever in hell
he was. Without him, I could not have survived."*
RAY BRADBURY

When Ray Bradbury was in the fourth grade, Buck Rogers comics came into his life. As he says in his book *Zen in the Art of Writing: Essays on Creativity*, it was "instant love." He was obsessed, captivated.

Shortly thereafter, his friends began to make fun of him and criticize his passion—so much so, he ended up tearing up his comics and abandoning them. For one long month, Bradbury walked around in a stupor, completely empty and sad. When he burst into tears, wondering what had happened to himself, he knew in an instant that, for him, life without Buck Rogers wasn't worth living.

He brought the comics back, and deemed his "friends" enemies. In so doing, Bradbury not only rescued the presence of the crucial, creative mulch in his life that ultimately gave birth to countless works of fiction, he also protected what I call his Joy Source. Many years later, he would marvel at his capacity at such a young age to rebel against social pressures.

For every Bradbury standing in defiance of what he loves, there are millions of souls gone early to their graves having bowed to peer or parental pressure.

Are you one of those souls?

Before you dismiss such a notion, I know from experience that it is easy to gloss over the insidious ways we stomped out the existence of our Joy Sources. Think back to all the things you did as a child or young adult that brought you happiness.

Was there something you used to love doing that is no longer a part of your life? Was there a hobby, a passion, a burning interest that got pushed aside when someone else—or you—deemed it frivolous?

Let's turn the clock back and capture any Joy Sources that may have been, consciously or unconsciously, cruelly quashed.

exercise Reclaiming Your Joy Sources

Take out your journal. At the top of the page, write "My Play History."

Think back to the top five most fun, exhilarating, and joyful experiences of your entire life. These were times you felt completely in flow, happy, fulfilled, connected, resonant, light in your body, and in your zone of ease. Write two paragraphs on each instance, quickly capturing the essence of what you were doing.

When you are finished, go back and circle all the verbs in each story. Make a list of them all.

When I did an exercise similar to this over thirty years ago while reading *What Color Is Your Parachute? A Practical Manual for Job-Hunters and Career-Changers* by Richard N. Bolles, my verb list looked like this:

- Wrote
- Led
- Created
- Taught
- Started

Over and over and over again, the same verbs appear throughout each of my play history stories. Each time I review this list, I'm always taken aback seeing how neatly and simply these five verbs capture the heart of what brings me alive.

What insights can you glean from your list? What do you think your play history is telling you? Is there something you parted with as a bow to peer or parental pressure? Is there something you stopped doing that sent a near-fatal wound to your delight?

If so, it is time to ignite your inner rebel and stand up for yourself.

· · · · ·

How you feel is your compass to changing your life. It is your first and best clue to begin unraveling where you are entangled, consciously or not. Author Martha Beck cautions us that our minds will tell us stories all day long, but our bodies will always tell us the truth. Check how resonant your play history verbs feel in your body. Do those verbs seem to vibrate with a certain truth even if it feels equal parts scary and exciting to consider bringing those actions back into your life?

Reclaim your Joy Sources. Renounce anything and anyone that keeps you from what you love. Step back into flow. Plant a flag. Take a stand. Call your true self back to yourself and come home to your birthright: the headwaters of your happiness and creativity.

We are bombarded from birth with messages, constraints, expectations, norms, and prisons not of our own making. The most rebellious act we can perform, becoming a creative rebel, is to live in accordance with our true selves and express ourselves fully to the world.

The Beginning of Remembering
· ·

"Half of life is lost in charming others. The other
half is lost in going through anxieties caused by others.
Leave this play. You have played enough."
RUMI

I gathered my dirty clothes into a ball and took them to the courtyard to wash. It was early summer in 1987, and the late-afternoon Lagos sun cast a golden glow, slanted on the walls of the Algarve housing complex. Laundry lines crisscrossed between the buildings, and a few shirts, towels, and socks flapped in the spring breeze.

I filled the stainless steel tub with my clothes, water, and powdered soap, plunged my hands into the grungy mass, and started churning and rubbing each item. It was the first time I had done laundry since my friends and I had embarked on our post–college graduation European adventure, and I was thrilled by the prospect of having fresh clothes.

Overhead, a radio was on; I couldn't understand the broadcaster's Portuguese, but I could tell by the periodic eruptions of cheers that their football team was in the lead.

I turned my attention to the clothesline. Out of nowhere, a strange surging, jolting shiver coursed through me, followed by one of the most delicious waves of bliss I had ever experienced.

The courtyard. The laundry lines. The ancient exterior walls of the buildings. The football game. The sounds of life coming from the windows all around me. The soft, balmy breeze with all of its edges rounded. The freedom of traveling with my friends. The newness of it all, though it felt eerily familiar, as if I had lived it before.

A homecoming.

"To rebel is to truly own your own self."

Dhani Harrison

As I rinsed the clothes and wrung them out, I was careful to stay connected to whatever had taken ahold of me. I did not want to lose it, scare it off. The buoyancy of the profound sense of connection, history, past and present rolled through me. It was as if I had found a twin I didn't know existed. A part of me that had been unknowingly lost up until then.

In that moment, I was taken from one level of awareness to a new understanding, to a deeper sense of my true nature. One moment I held a certain perspective, and in the next, it was exploded open into a connection to my heart.

It was the beginning of what poet David Whyte calls reconnecting with our "elemental waters," a concept introduced to him by Benedictine monk Brother David Steindl-Rast. This is a place of belonging where we are reconnected with our own grace, carrying us forward with ease. It is the place that brings us alive with the very people we want to adventure with, in the very way we want to work and be.

When entrepreneurs and creators come to me for coaching, they are often caught in the undertow of the Stagnation Zone, stuck in some weird limbo of anxiety and frustration. They have run out of steam and can no longer find meaning in their business or personal lives, or connection with their market.

Whatever they used to propel themselves forward in the past is no longer working, and they are at a painful crossroads. It is a powerful moment of choice: They can rise to a new level of self or stay stuck and witness their enterprise falter and fizzle out.

While getting bogged down in the Stagnation Zone is scary, it is filled with untold possibility. Like my moment in Portugal, it can be the beginning of remembering one's elemental waters. An awakening. A call to a new horizon.

And if the entrepreneur is willing to not know the destination or how things will unfold along the way, they will rise to a new level of self. This provides the raw material for breaking free, returning to joy, reclaiming your creativity, healing old hurts, and finding market fit and business growth.

In Portugal, I realized my life was connected to something I had never known. A horizon I didn't know was even there. It was another message in a bottle, a riddle for me to break apart and attempt to decipher. It was a nudge to learn much more about exploring inklings and not tune them out. It was the beginning of understanding there was much more to me and what brought me alive than I had realized.

We are called over and over from within ourselves to wake up. Often, we choose to hit the snooze button on our lives, preferring routine and familiarity, regardless of how painful they are.

Clients will often tell me they do not know their true purpose or passion. This is a fear-based lie we tell ourselves. We do know. We just have forgotten how to remember.

exercise Energy Levels and Elemental Waters

Consider your level of energy right now. Your energetic state usually reflects the amount of time you spend in your own elemental waters. Where are you lumbering and struggling against your true self? Where are you fully in grace and ease? Add these questions into your journal and take ten minutes to write a few lines answering both.

As we remove the tasks, mindsets, ways of working, habits, people, and environments that are non-elemental waters for us, we will feel an all-encompassing lightness rising within us. This work requires many "passes," as it is not a one-and-done effort.

We can choose the path that requires more courage up front, like a deposit into the account of our future self. Little by little, we can ease down into our elemental waters and return to experiencing more of what brings us resonant joy in each moment.

Truth-Telling as the Art of Living

"Depart from your truth in any way—offer a fake smile, flatter your awful boss, marry for money—and you become two people: the truth knower and the lie actor."
MARTHA BECK

All entrepreneurs and creators have known the pain and frustration of being stuck—unable to find the right words, the flowing zone of ease—when attempting to get what is in their heads onto paper in a clear and compelling way.

Austin Kleon, who describes himself as a writer who draws, has a simple way to combat such trudges through the quicksand. When he gets stuck on a writing project, he will stop and ask himself one powerful question: *What did you really want to say?*

Ever since I came across this golden nugget, I have wielded it against some of my thorniest writing challenges. I have been relieved to discover that pausing to ask myself this question helps chisel out the substance of what it is I want to convey, the way Michelangelo liberated figures from marble.

But what if the words we are laying down are hollow? Incomplete? Not clear enough? And worst of all, what if what we are writing is not totally honest?

We do it all the time. Little shavings off the truth here and there. Choosing to stop ourselves from writing *that*, saying *this*, or going *there*. Keeping our words safe, more flattering to ourselves. Opting out of vulnerability and visibility, embracing instead a well-padded, beige, boring sameness so we don't stand apart or risk being viewed negatively.

I was incredibly struck by how writer, director, and producer Brian Koppelman presented himself during an interview on the *Tim Ferriss Show*. Throughout the entire conversation, Brian took great care to be very clear that he wanted no daylight between his private and public selves.

Every time he felt he was edging out of total integrity and truth-telling, he'd stop himself and correct the record, even when what he was pointing out was not particularly flattering. Over and over and over, he revealed deeply personal aspects of his life, how he now chooses to approach the conversations he has with others, and how he presents himself to the world.

With every truth, every reveal, I was drawn in deeper and deeper into the layers of meaning. I was riveted, inspired, and energized, not only by the content of their discussion but also by how Brian made sure that each one of his words reflected a profound honesty.

Now when I get to critical points in my writing, I'll stop and ask myself two questions:

1 What did you really want to say?
2 Is it honest?

I'll dig to reveal where I am holding myself back. Where I have a gap of any size between my private and public selves. Where I'm holding my reader at bay while I hide behind a fabrication, large or small. I bring my inner Brian Koppelman to the page, along with my courage to write the things that scare me most in sharing.

Our readers, listeners, and ideal clients can intuit when we are faking it instead of telling the truth, digging down to the marrow and sharing it all—the good, bad, embarrassing, and ugly.

Our courage breaks open something in the reader and us. It connects us to more genuine living and being. The transformative power of truth-telling lifts others and stirs them awake.

When we stop holding ourselves back, we model the dual powers of possibility and authenticity.

We link arms with our readers and clients, landing together on the space on the game board labeled freedom and genuine, inspiring connection.

Creative Incubation and Your Identity

"You must have a room, or a certain hour or so a day, where you don't know what was in the newspapers that morning, . . . who your friends are, . . . what you owe anybody, . . . what anybody owes to you."
JOSEPH CAMPBELL

Joan Rivers worked nonstop her whole life, terrified that if she were to ever pause or take time off, someone would take her place. In a documentary on the comedian, *Joan Rivers: A Piece of Work*, there is a scene in which Joan lifts her blank planner to the camera and says, "I'll show you fear. That's fear."

If you were to open your planner or digital calendar right now, how much "white space" would you see? Is every moment accounted for, including your downtime? And if so, is that feeling both comforting and frustrating?

We have become incredibly efficient in making sure we fill our lives so intensely that we literally do not have time to think. Yet, it is no secret that the pace is slowly eroding our joy in life, as well as in our relationships and creativity.

But there is another casualty in this self-created culture of constant "on": there is no space to learn who we are.

Most of my clients believe they know who they are (at least initially) and are quick to rattle off what they do for a living as evidence. I then ask them again who they are, searching deeper into their hearts and souls—probing for what they love, what makes their heart sing, what brings them to their knees in sadness, what disgusts them, what breaks their hearts, and what connects them to the deepest and most joyful parts of themselves. That is when the look of bewilderment, followed by panic, shows in their faces.

As Joseph Campbell demonstrated, for us to reconnect to ourselves and rekindle our creativity, we need a sacred place to retreat to—a place that is quiet and free of distractions. Author and researcher Joe Dispenza calls this becoming (paradoxically) no one, in no place, in no time. This sacred space can be a physical place of refuge and quiet or a meditative practice like walking in the woods alone or sitting for an extended meditation.

We have to meet the uncomfortable silence and the not doing. Our ego will wage a war at this point, in a desperate attempt to stay relevant. The only way to move beyond it is to move through it. To do so, you must surrender and stay the course with courage.

On other side of this Creative Rebel's Voyage you will find the most divine memory of your authentic self and evidence of the vast, unlimited creativity you possess.

exercise Spotting Patterns in What Stops You in Your Tracks

The day I sketched peaches for the first time was the day I realized how little of the world I noticed. I sensed the depth and opaqueness of the fog I perpetually walked around in, always thinking about the next thing to cross off my to-do list in a futile attempt to never feel behind. When I sat in that art studio with my sketch pad on my lap, I grieved the loss of letting so much slip by—unnoticed, unseen, unappreciated. How many moments of wonder and delight had I euthanized as I raced from appointment to appointment, galloping toward another client meeting, another deal?

In his book *Several Short Sentences about Writing*, author and academic Verlyn Klinkenborg asserts: "If you notice something, it's because it's important." As entrepreneurs and creators, if we are to touch the edges of what we are truly capable of, we must amp our authority to create way up. Klinkenborg suggests that we do this by paying attention to what interests us and the "shape and meaning of [our] own thoughts."

Take yourself on a leisurely stroll and bring your journal and pen with you. What interests you? What captures your attention? What stops you midstride? Can you spot a pattern in these moments of arresting noticing? What is it? Write it all down.

Once you have returned home, think back to the most compelling articles, essays, and books you have read over the last several months. The movies you have seen. The poetry you have heard. The art you have let yourself get lost in. The conversations that piqued your interest. The lectures or podcasts that ignited a firestorm of ideas within you. The music that moved you to dance or to tears. Which experiences fascinated you? Why? What subject matter has you by the tail with excitement these days? Take a few moments and write down your answers and thoughts.

5

Protecting and Fueling Your Creative Energy

"Energy and persistence conquer all things."

BENJAMIN FRANKLIN

WHEN I was in the first grade, I threw up every day before school. I was painfully shy, an introvert afraid of just about everything and everyone. Oddly, though, I loved school. When our teacher, Ms. Brown, stood at the blackboard and explained a lesson, I didn't take my eyes or attention off her. My body buzzed when my brain was pushed and stretched.

I could feel something inside me powering on as I retrieved my pencil out of the well-worn and darkened groove at the top of the wooden desk. I'd dig into working problems and completing exercises with utter delight. I touched something new when I learned. I could see the edge pieces forming the outline of the vast universe of all the things I didn't know yet, thrilled by the challenge of filling in and revealing the image of the completed puzzle. And those school supplies? Don't even get me started. My obsession continues in its full glory to this day.

So why was my tummy and every emotion in such an uproar each morning? Why did I feel so anxious about being in an environment that I truly enjoyed?

It wasn't until I was in my twenties that I began to understand. On a lark, I attended a gathering of palm readers in Boston one afternoon. I had no idea what to expect. I was curious to know what my outstretched palm would show. Could this woman seated across from me, wearing a turtleneck and sporting a gray ponytail, looking more like a librarian than a palm reader, tell me of great adventures in my future? Boundless love? Fortune? Long life?

She cradled my hand in hers and gazed downward. She immediately looked up at me over the top of her glasses with eyes soft with kindness and understanding. It turned out she had a warning for me.

"Susie, listen to me," she said. "You must be very, very careful about who you are around. I can see just how much you soak up the energy of everyone you are near... good and bad. There will be some people who will gravitate toward you because of your light. They will seek your energy as their own and will drain you. Choose your company with the greatest of care."

My light-hearted approach to an afternoon palm-reading session had turned heavy, foreboding. I was scared at first by what she told me. It felt like a weird curse that doomed me to a life of warding off toxic vibes and energy vampires.

I walked through Boston's Back Bay streets and cobblestone sidewalks, trying to sort out what the palm reader had said. The closer I got to my apartment in Beacon Hill, the more I realized the magnitude of the gift that the woman with the kind eyes had given me. She had imparted ancient knowledge that would continue to reveal its power to me over the decades.

With each block, more and more things started to make sense. I thought back to times when, for no apparent reason, I had felt depleted, foggy, on edge, off balance. This particular relationship, that colleague, this friend, that group, this experience, that party, this job.

The palm reader had given me the Rosetta Stone for unlocking energy's impact on my every thought, feeling, and action.

Thinking back to my experience in the first grade, I realized I had been absorbing all the other little energies in the room, and it was completely overwhelming and disorienting.

It threw my entire system into a swirling mess. Each morning, when I anticipated that energy landing, it made me nauseated.

Much later, I would learn that there is a word for people who, like me, deeply experience the emotions of others and are so highly tuned to them that they absorb their energy into their own: empath. The more I understand the energetic fields we possess, the more I think we are all empaths, to some degree or another.

Protecting our energy is our most important job. Doing so is vital for not just our imaginative powers but also our overall well-being. We begin by noticing where we have flimsy or non-existent boundaries and work our way forward to auditing and changing our depleting habits. We learn the power of making and keeping promises to ourselves.

The way to bring out the best in ourselves is to remember that our job is to be a calming presence for that fearful, anxious creator that lives within each of us. The goal is not to be more efficient or productive. We achieve both when we put down our clipboards and place our uneasy bodies into playpens of various shapes and sizes.

When we hold back on overbooking, overdoing, and stretching ourselves to exhaustion, we release our outdated attachments to apprehension and open up space that ushers in the energy required for the creative work we are truly in love with.

Similarly, when we see the lie of the promise of multitasking and frenetic task switching, we regain our agency over our creative powers and clarity. The calm, natural state we deserve. Each time we hop from one task to another, like a rabbit chasing clover in a spring field, our intelligence wanes, as do our reserves for staying in the work that requires our best thinking and courage. Our presence and powers of awareness tremble and fall like leaves loosened in autumn wind.

This is especially true when we are engaged in work that offers a neural pendulum swing from a state of creating to one of strategic thinking or editing. The energy cost between those two swings is vast and hard to detect on a conscious level. We may vaguely perceive an annoyance, like a fluorescent bulb flickering or buzzing in the background, but not be aware of its insidious, relentless misting on our creative fire.

We need stretches of buffer time before we go into creative work and again after we are finished. We'll naturally underestimate the amount of time we need, so double or triple what your first instinct tells you and gift that to yourself.

Note that we can, in a perverse way, enjoy the distance from our creativity that multitasking and overdoing offers us. The energy pooling at our feet is our safe harbor from judgment and vulnerability. Simply being aware of our tendency to dance with invisibility can help us ensure we are not hiding from our creativity by euthanizing it through actively depleting our energy.

We can safeguard our vulnerable hearts while remaining engaged in our work. We can tend to our creative fire with kindling sticks of quiet, focus, and protected time.

We cannot revel in the rich depths of inspiration if we aren't first willing to dig a protective moat around our creative energy. Only then can we offer our work to the world, while lifting our chins and risking rejection or criticism.

More Mister Rogers (Less Hustle and Slay)

During the winters of my early childhood, our family would pack up the station wagon and make the long drive to Key Largo, Florida. After two days in the car, we were rewarded by spotting the mile markers on Overseas Highway, which we counted down to Snug Harbor, my grandparents' home on the bay.

It was a true tropical paradise. I spent my days fishing, swimming, climbing over mangrove roots, searching for drift-wood, and studying the grotesque yet fascinating underbellies of horseshoe crabs. In the afternoons, I'd finally go inside for a late lunch. I'd roll the giant ottoman in front of the television, eat a bologna sandwich, and watch *Mister Rogers' Neighbor-hood*. My favorite meal, my favorite show, in my favorite place in the entire world.

I loved the softness, the sweet gentleness of the show, and how its predictable rhythms and routines echoed the ease of daily life during Key Largo winters. Mister Rogers told me every afternoon that I was special and loved. That I had value and worth just by being myself. His calm voice and demeanor encouraged me to follow my curiosity and seek out adven-tures. For a child who tended to run high on anxiety and fear, he was a soothing balm on my soul, like aloe on my sunburned shoulders.

I recently polled my friends to learn their perspective of Mister Rogers and how he had influenced their lives. The responses were consistent across the board: he was a calming, loving presence who beautifully modeled unconditional love.

Mister Rogers could see the Golden Buddha version of us and continued to call us to live in accord with our truth, reveal-ing what is unique and special about ourselves.

So, what does Mister Rogers have to do with our adult lives and our creativity? If you are like me, you have grown weary of what I call the current "Hustle and Slay" culture of entre-preneurship. The amped-up thought leaders and coaches with cups of coffee in their hands, admonishing us to whip our inner wusses into submission and make those seven figures by the end of the fourth quarter.

Push, push, push. Drive, drive, drive. Discipline, damn it!

And as our mirror neurons pick up on all that cortisol and adrenaline, our minds dart around, looking in a panic for the things we should be doing. Rather than being settled into ourselves, working from a place of calm confidence, we are frantically striving, with the dreaded sense that we are not enough.

If the path we must follow requires such relentless effort, if we're going to get our asses kicked every step of the way, we must be starting out this journey missing what it takes to succeed, right?

Nothing could be further from the truth. Yes, the path can be challenging, and sometimes downright gut wrenching. Yet we are already enough before we begin. The way to bring out the best in ourselves is to remember to be Mister Rogers for that fearful, anxious creator who exists in us. We coax ourselves forward with unconditional love while letting the invisible shutters that keep us from doing great work—Resistance—gently open and close. Fear-based action only creates more resistance.

Ideas need to simmer and percolate into maturity. The best way to transcend our myriad blocks is by entering new states of being that quiet our racing mind, not inflame it. Relentless push creates equal pushback, not real progress or the mining of the untold riches of our unique, creative power.

I think I know why we tend to work as if someone were chasing us with a whip. This relentless pushing forward is an effective strategy to swat away the naysaying blurts emanating from the scared, small parts of us. We love our work ethic, our strategic mind, and our enviable ability to get more done in three hours than others do in three days.

This ongoing striving, striving, and never arriving, though, comes with a hefty price: discomfort in the center of our gut that judges lack of not just progress, but *perfect* progress.

Sometimes taking a nap is the best battery for sparking your creativity.

By healing and loving ourselves (just as Mister Rogers modeled for us), we cross the chasm and transcend the parts of us that have long been stuck—the old mindsets and emotions that rear up when we decide to get going, try something new, or present with our vulnerable voice. In becoming our fully creative selves, we embrace our ultimate, enduring transformation.

We meet the challenges in front of us, believing, knowing, we are enough.

exercise On Boundaries and Drains

Take a moment now and journal your answers to these questions: What is bleeding into you? What are you bleeding into others? For example, where do you allow your boundaries to become porous, and what are the nonnegotiable values and desires you routinely dilute, compromise, and pretend do not exist? Where might you be pressuring others to leave behind their sure footing in the center of themselves to adopt a camouflage to neatly fit with you, so as to not disturb your balance?

As you begin to formulate and understand your answers, return to inhabiting your body fully. That is, don't fall prey to the trap of continuing to distract yourself, distancing yourself from the emotions coursing through your body. How you are feeling is your biggest indicator of when you are inching up on what is true for you.

Do not ignore your feelings or intuition. Your mind may tell you stories about why you should date a certain person, join a particular group, get more done each day, take the alluring job, or hire the seemingly talented assistant, all the while ignoring your misgivings. Your heart knows better. Listen to it.

Now that you have begun the work of seeing where you need stronger boundaries to protect your creative energy, let's look at practical methods you can employ when you need more definition between you and others, patching any energy leaks that are draining you.

This list is not exhaustive, but let it serve as a starting place for your energy leak audit.

- If you are feeling off, edgy, or icky before a planned interaction with someone, stop and let all the feelings come through. Ask your intuition for insight into your feelings. Do not override your intuition; most likely, there's something to unpack and understand.

- If you are in a meeting and things go off the rails (that is, someone's energy is consuming you), and your brain has gone offline as a result, stop and call for a brief break. Separate from the others and find a place where you can be alone to collect yourself, jump-start your brain, and get back in the saddle as the pack leader of your own energy.

- If you have an energy hangover after leaving a certain person or experience, journal what happened. Look for clues. Is this a one-off occurrence or chronic?

- Examine the creative projects you desire to complete. How much time have you dedicated to doing the work required? Have you arranged any buffer days before or afterward? Be honest. If you don't have enough ramp-up or cool-down time around the creative work, rearrange or, even better, delegate or delete tasks.

- Can you spot any edgy pushing for productivity in your planner? If so, can you surface what you may be avoiding doing, thinking, or feeling?

• • • • •

Remember, if you have something calling to your heart to create and you continue to engage with activities and people who make you feel bad, you may be using the interaction to numb out or self-sabotage instead of doing the risky, creative work. Hiding out from the world and our own creative force can offer an appealing and painful cocktail. We can throw distraction, interruption of thought, and numbing out into the shaker and slug it down just as we are approaching a creative breakthrough. Creativity often happens in the background of our thinking, as ideas, insights, and information bump into each other in chance encounters, eventually forming little, sprouting buds. But those seeds cannot take root if we continue to disrupt the fertile soil.

WHEN DARREN came to me for help in a creative slump, I asked him what his typical workday looked like. As he rattled off a sample day of admin and accounting tasks, client calls and meetings, picking up kids after school, and then finally sitting down at his desk late in the day to try to design stunning interiors, it was more than clear he was starving himself of time to think. Five or more hours of his day were packed to the gills with draining work and errands. No wonder that when he reached into the bucket of creativity for his design work, it was empty. He was on a gerbil wheel of other people's agendas during the key creative hours of the day.

Darren's work had become generic. He was worried that he'd lost his desire to do it and had even considered abandoning his career entirely. His client pipeline had dried up, so he was scrambling to attract new business to keep his company afloat. This anxiety further removed him from what inspired him and added drudgery to even the work that lit him up.

We worked together to rearrange his week. His first assignment was to clear his weekend of work so that he began his Mondays after two buffer days spent resting, enjoying his family, and soaking up activities that fueled his imagination. Then we blocked out a day and a half for all his client meetings and calls. He hired a virtual assistant to handle his admin and accounting tasks and joined a parent carpool so he only had to pick up the kids after school one afternoon a week.

Darren's week now had three full days of creating. Well-rested, clear, and in control, his heart and creative output soared. Six months later, he won a coveted design award, and word of his inventive and exciting interiors once again spread like wildfire. When Darren had more business than he could handle, he raised his rates and enjoyed doing only the design work he was most interested in doing.

Learn what it feels like to be only in your energy for extended periods of time. See how that impacts your creativity, as well as your courage and willingness to create. Notice the increase of creative connection among ideas that you may have tucked away in a forgotten book on the corner shelf. Find your old hiding spot inside the dusty volume and read your old notes.

If we entangle ourselves in energy that confuses, saddens, and depletes us, the creative force within us dims to a pale, dying ember. If we choose instead to hold loving boundaries for ourselves, focusing on protecting our sacred energy, we can connect to the divine in powerful ways that forge our creative energy into works that change worlds.

We cannot express the poetry of what we find unique and captivating about the world if we haven't taken a hoe to the weeds choking our creative energy. If we haven't let ourselves crawl into the cotton sheets of feeling it all, or done what feels unnatural at first: show up for what is ours and ours alone.

Ideas that are destined to visit us will refuse to land if we haven't steadied and shored up our tender, creative power.

Getting Sober Everywhere

In the fall of 2020, I stopped drinking alcohol. Cold turkey. I finally had had enough of the wonky sleep, poor food choices, and fuzzy thinking during my peak morning hours.

Most nights, I'd have one to three glasses of wine to end the day and draw a line between being "on duty" and "off." In the middle of a day that was especially frustrating, I'd often fast-forward in my mind to that moment when I could settle in after my workday with a great glass of wine and let it all melt away.

I came to realize, however, that my habit had an insidious cost, especially to my creativity. I began to notice that on the days following the evenings when I chose not to drink, I felt lighter, more focused, more eager to conquer challenging creative work. I had courage to dive into the unknown when writing and give it a go. Creative heaven for a writer.

Conversely, my mornings with a slight hangover had a film of fatigue, fuzziness, and dropped connections. I would stand at my French press, stare into the coffee grounds, and start to run the questions: "What was I thinking again about that idea? What was the interesting point there? Shit! It was so good! What was it?"

I also noticed something else I find hard to admit: my drinking consumed precious courage reserves and sense-of-self bandwidth. Without fail, during the mornings after the wine, I would run a shame program in the background. It

"That is a normal
part of creativity—
letting go."

Julia Cameron

encouraged my doubt and gave fuel and center stage to my inner critic.

Wine also robbed me of my best thinking and creative energy hours: 3 a.m. to 10 a.m. So, I began contemplating my relationship with alcohol and whether I should reconsider drinking altogether.

My journal was filled with a running litany of reasons why I should stop drinking, as well as why I could continue without harm. It wasn't a problem. It was a problem. Back and forth. Back and forth.

I decided to run an experiment. I would stop drinking until I had finished the first draft of my book. Eight months without alcohol—enough time to be a useful, longitudinal study.

The results were fascinating. Along with more consistent and restful sleep, I enjoyed greater clarity, improved concentration, and better overall health. I no longer snacked before dinner, and I ate healthier meals. Not much of a surprise.

What *was* surprising to me was the power of making and keeping promises to myself. The simple act of deciding, making a commitment to myself, and honoring that commitment proved to be a true game changer for my creativity. Commitment begets commitment. Continuity begets continuity. Showing up fully for myself created more of the same throughout my entire life.

Breaking the habit that held me in a loose yet draining grip liberated pockets of energy, insight, thoughtfulness, and grace within me.

Are you consuming something that is causing a latent drag in your creativity? Maybe for you, too, alcohol is a buffer that slices two ways. Of course, our culture is loaded with lore about how drinking eases us into creativity more readily. Alcohol and creativity, as it turns out, are not a good mix for most of us.

Maybe it isn't alcohol for you. Maybe it is a toxic relationship or a junk food habit that makes you feel leaden, sluggish. Or a day job that is sucking the life out of you. Or perhaps it is a choice to work all the time, separating yourself from rest, joy, or playful adventure. Perhaps, like I did, you have more than one habit that is weighing you down.

The dulled version of me was steeped in pain and isolation. Unable to access what makes me unique. My unhealthy habits of overeating, overdrinking, and overworking dimmed my internal power source, my creativity mitochondria. Snuffed out my willingness to show up as a person of agency. Setting myself free readied me to march forward, amplified and unapologetic.

When I finished the first draft of this book, I began a new experiment. I wondered if I would be able to enjoy a glass of wine without using it as a way not to feel. Could I have wine on occasion, like a dessert, and let it be a celebratory moment instead of a choice to wall myself off from myself? Or would wine just have to remain off limits?

As it turned out, wine was no longer a deadening force in my life. I could have a glass while out with friends or at a special dinner at one of my favorite restaurants and not need for it to be a numbing-out agent. The strange dance between drinking and me was over. I could take or leave it without thinking about it too much or feeling regret in my body. The wild swings had ceased, and the pendulum was still and at center. By mindfully crossing the chasm of hiding and not feeling over to visibility and feeling everything, I completely stripped alcohol and all of my other previous crutches of their edgy power.

I will never return to a mindless cycle of numbing out via any substance, habit, or choice. The clear and empowered energy I have now feels too good to relinquish. Waking early to do The 5Ms sends me on a collision course with serendipity, inspiration, and calm every day. I am simply not willing to separate myself from experiencing the entirety of who I am, what I am capable of creating, and the heights and depths of being human, fully immersed in the world.

exercise Your Numbing Agents

How about we bring the choices and habits that are causing latent drags on our creativity right up front and center? Let's take a good, long look there. Take a few minutes to think through your numbing agents of choice and write about your discoveries in your journal. What kind of experiment can you run, beginning today, that may prove to be the decision that, once and for all, sets you free?

If you choose to make one change, begin tracking the results in your journal. Capture how you feel and how your behavior is or is not changing. Think and write, too, about this notion of how kept promises and courageous choices build our sense of self in powerful, mystical ways. Is your experiment unlocking you and your creativity? If so, in what ways? Do you see evidence of your decision rippling through other areas of your personal life and business? Write it all down.

Discipline and Desire

. . . .

"Discipline is much easier when it's fueled by desire."
AUSTIN KLEON

Lynn texted me and asked for an emergency coaching session. She said she was having a breakdown or a breakthrough, or maybe both.

When she answered the phone, I could hear in her voice that she had been crying.

"I've been working so hard for so long, trying and trying. Everything in my business and my life feels broken. Out of control. I'm frustrated, sad, and tired! Something has to change now!"

I told her that I absolutely understood the fatigue, worry, and anxiety she was going through and knew how much pain she was in.

"Let's start with what you *do* want," I said.

"That's one of the problems! I don't know what I want! It's like I can't even remember who I am." She began to cry again.

We talked for a little over an hour. I walked her back in time to reveal that she did, in fact, know what she wanted. What brought her immense joy. She could remember after all.

She ached for the serenity of a long solo walk along the shore, where she could spot birds wading in tidal pools, study the lush plants that almost overpowered the trails along the marsh, and sit in the sand and stare at waves collapsing into themselves. She missed taking photographs of misty mornings, rock jetties, and children digging with plastic shovels. She yearned to feel the sense of balance in her body, being at home in her own skin, that came from being immersed in salt air, lost in thought. She craved the delicious feeling of being pelted with ideas and the electricity of considering possibilities.

Our conversation and her willingness to remember what brought her joy was a very good start to her reclaiming what she craved in her life and bringing it closer. Once we let ourselves down onto the raft that carries us to that buoyant state we are desperate for, we find that what we seek is precisely what we have chosen to let slide through our fingers like the end of a rope attached to our former selves.

Six weeks after our conversation, Lynn had returned to the shoreline of herself. She was no longer withholding the places, activities, and states of mind that powered her soul. She made sure that she spent long stretches of time in places where she came alive, doing the things that she loved to do. From this energized state of being, Lynn stirred and rejuvenated the creative cauldron within. We then began working on making changes in her business that similarly reflected what it was she wanted most.

Lynn's situation is not unique. Many of my entrepreneur clients are experiencing this amnesia when we first begin working together. Why is this so common?

We are trained from an early age to focus intensely on what is not desired. *Hot stove! Corner of coffee table! Don't eat that!* As we become teenagers, the yellow caution flags thrown onto the field in front of us change shape: *You can't skip going to college! You can't make a living doing XYZ!* Later, as young adults on our own, the vigilant cries morph yet again: *Start-up businesses consistently fail! You can't love or marry so-and-so!*

Of course, these kinds of warnings from parents, teachers, peers, and culture tend to come from well-meaning hearts—hearts, though, that have grown dim and fearful from hearing the same piercing tweets throughout their own lives.

As a result, if we are not filled with an unrelenting and courageous desire to forge ahead toward our own heart's desires, we can become numb, confused about what it is we do want, wrapped in a cloak of powerlessness over our own destiny.

We can become supremely talented at studying the eyes of others for clues that our choices are within bounds, smart. Safe. We make decisions without consulting our souls, dark and walled off in the basement of ourselves, behind a door shut and bolted at the top of the stairs.

Eventually, the trail leading us to living in accord with our true selves grows over, leaving only a faint line that disappears in shadows and reappears, teasing us, on days when the sun is especially bright.

When we've traveled this far from our essential nature, it can take Herculean efforts to do the smallest tasks. We may say we have lost our mojo, our magic. We might lean into procrastination, avoiding the work to build our business, or stop creating altogether and choose to hide. At this point, well-intending others may suggest that perhaps we just lack discipline.

No.

What we lack is *desire*.

Our desires are our innate discipline. We routinely turn off the oxygen supply to our desires, and then we try to whip ourselves into being motivated to produce more and better work and results. And then we worry and wonder why we've failed.

How do we find our way back to the desire to create anything we want?

We return to whatever fills the well of inspiration for us. To whatever feels like play. To the work we'd do all day for free because it connects us powerfully to joy and brings us alive. We put down obligation and duty. We remember to protect our sacred energy. We shore up our boundaries and put our agenda first for once. We move our bodies in fresh air and gift ourselves restorative, unplugged time. We allow ourselves quiet to reflect, remember what has been calling to our hearts. Something that may seem frivolous, perhaps too wild. An adventure.

exercise Your Gifts to Yourself

What will you choose as your gifts to yourself? How will you decide to close the gap between where you are now and the future you hunger for? How will you amp up desire?

Take a moment right now and remember what it is you really want. What is your commitment to inspiration? Add your thoughts in your journal.

Your mojo is closer than you think.

The Cure for Anxiety and Overdoing: The 7-Inch Plate

"Let everything happen to you: beauty and terror.
Just keep going. No feeling is final."
RAINER MARIA RILKE

My anxiety is a six-foot green monster that sits in the corner of each room, knitting a long, "Thneed"-like garment. It sits, knits, looks up occasionally at me to stare disapprovingly, and knits some more. Long needles clack-clack as the yarn works. The monster messages me telepathically: *Why that and not this? Humph! Good luck pulling that off. Who do you think you are? Seriously? Get going. It's not enough. You're not enough. Why aren't you moving? Get busy, soldier!*

Clack, clack, clack go the needles.

When I stop being present and aware in the moment, I let anxiety overtake my sense of self, my thoughts, my direction. I try to outrun those monster messages by being supremely busy. In go-go-go mode, I don't hear the needles clacking. When I look up, exhausted and spent, I'll see the monster over in the corner, but it has shrunk in size and is starting to nod off. It will grow to its hideous height again in the morning, refreshed and ready to resume its onslaught.

I'll be ready, though. I'll write my dissertation of tomorrow's tasks before stopping work for the day. Most likely, I'll let that heap of work consume my thoughts overnight, simmering in the cauldron of my mind and disrupting any chance of truly restorative sleep.

As entrepreneurs and creators, it is easy for us to fall prey to the anxiety monster. We scrutinize others' enterprises and works and wonder if we are far enough along. Doing the right things. Creative enough. Talented enough. Others' worlds seem so much more together than ours. We feel shabby, disorganized, and overwhelmed when we steep ourselves in comparison mode.

And like wild horses, once we feed the monster that first crappy thought, it and we are off and running. Oh, the lengths we will go to avoid feeling.

As we bolt from the fire within, though, we disconnect from *all* feelings, not just the unpleasant ones. *Poof!* goes joy, inspiration, peace, curiosity, wonder, and connection with beauty, nature, and love.

This disconnect renders us dull, isolated. It prompts us to take up buffering behaviors to numb out the resulting pain: too much work, too much food and alcohol, not enough self-care. How, then, do we break the cycle and make peace with our demons, ourselves?

A couple of months ago, one of my entrepreneur clients came to see me amid a full-on battle with the anxiety monster. She was exhausted, off her healthy habits and routines, and feeling a brutal combination of despondency and worthlessness even though she was packing each moment of her day and working herself to a nub.

As she spoke, I received a wholly formed download of a wickedly effective coaching tool that I call The 7-Inch Plate. The second it came to my mind, I knew it was the perfect antidote for both my clients and me. Here is how it works:

If you have ever worked to lose weight, you've probably read about the benefit of eating off a smaller plate. This purportedly tricks the brain into thinking you are eating more food than you actually are, thereby fooling the stomach into feeling fuller.

Now let's apply this same concept to our energy, focus, and attention. Let's say that the typical amount of energy we need to do our work is the size of a twelve-inch plate. If we are in "outrun anxiety" mode, we will pile tasks and activities onto that plate like a teenage boy at a buffet, squeezing in more and more, so there's no blank space on our calendars. This mutes the anxiety temporarily while also suppressing our creative verve.

But if we were to trick ourselves into believing we had a seven-inch plate instead of a twelve-inch one, we'd hold back on overbooking and overdoing. *We'd leave room for creativity, pleasure, rest, exercise; surprises in our professional and personal lives; time for loved ones, nature, hobbies, and hearing ourselves think.*

We'd feel "full" without gorging ourselves on doing, doing, doing.

Note that it is dullness, a lack of creative expression, that makes us stack way too much work on our plates. Without our connection to inspiration and creativity, we muddle forward, piling on work in search of an adrenaline rush in a continual quest for the sense of completeness.

It's not unlike what drives us to overeat bland food. When we choose hollow, tasteless carbs, we eat but remain hungry, unsatisfied. What we truly desire is to savor something that fills us and transports us, like a dark chocolate ganache truffle from Paris's La Maison du Chocolat or a sun-ripened summer tomato plucked from the vine. In its absence, we stuff our schedules and ourselves.

Here is how one of my clients described her experience of transformation with this tool:

The 7-Inch Plate is a way of stepping away and looking at the portions of things I was doing. I was filling up every second of my day with activities and tasks I felt were productive (since productivity is where I put a lot of my own self-worth).

When I then looked at my days ... rather than filling up every second, I left extra blank spaces (like small bites) such as fifteen minutes between work meetings, nights without planned dinners, extra time to get ready, etc.

At first it was hard because there were times I wanted to "fit" more things in there ... but what I quickly realized is that the extra time then gave me three important things I didn't have before:

1   It allowed more room for errors; if things went wrong, a meeting ran late, or I didn't feel well, I was not desperately running to the next thing.

2   I started to truly appreciate the extra time and gave myself some sweet, extra moments for quiet reading or a walk that was not planned.

3   I started putting way less weight in the "productivity = self-worth" bucket because I became more compassionate and loving toward myself.

Every one of my hard-charging entrepreneur clients has reported incredible benefits from adopting The 7-Inch Plate tool into their lives and businesses. As for me, it has brought light to my creative expression, health, and sense of self. If you tend to turn the dial down on anxiety by overworking, give this tool a try. Let me know how it goes!

We can choose to live sumptuous lives, gleefully letting everything happen to us (as Rilke suggests)—letting in all the colors, emotions, and experiences of having a whole-hearted, open approach to each day. Knowing that no feeling is final, we can have the courage to feel each one, all the way through.

When we lower our inner drawbridges and stop barricading ourselves from feeling, we gift ourselves the protection of our sacred energy—the seat of our creativity and well-being.

exercise What Are Your Real Goals?

Write down all the goals you are feverish with getting done right now. After you have listed them, do a gut check. Are you racing down the wrong field? That is, when you picture your arrival on the other side of the finish line, are you elated and feeling aligned deep within your soul? Or are you a bit nauseated by the waste of your time and effort, wondering who you were trying to please?

Spend a few minutes and write your answers in your journal.

Gaining clarity on what we want to happen versus what we think we must do is job one for entrepreneurs as we discern what is important to us and our businesses.

inspiration beacon

TAKE YOURSELF on a solo Shadow Stroll. Set out on a gentle walk without your phone and spend thirty minutes completely absorbed in studying the size, shape, and movement of the shadows that surround you. Notice how they shift, dance, change. Drop completely into their patterns, how they elongate and shorten. How they come into view and then leave your periphery. Do a thirty-second sketch of a shadow that captures your attention. Quickly draw its essence in your journal and make a brief note about why you noticed it.

6

The
Provenance of
Becoming

"Be a provenance of something gathered, a summation of previous intuitions."

DAVID WHYTE

"I'VE GOT a hard stop at ten today," Nate said. "Just a heads-up. Back-to-back meetings all day."

I could hear his labored breathing through the phone and knew he was out on a powerwalk.

"Gotcha," I said. "We'll wrap up a couple of minutes before the hour."

Every time Nate reminded me of his jam-packed schedule, I cringed a little. I remembered wearing that "crazy busy" merit badge with pride too. And how it almost destroyed my life. Working fifteen hours a day, steeping my body in a soup of cortisol and anxiety. Competing against a hologram, my image of the successful entrepreneur. Always pushing to send one more email, make one more call, before I gifted myself a brief break. Stashing little piles of work so I'd never run out. On the rare occasions I slowed my frenetic pace, the sadness and punishing thoughts I was so desperate to avoid came rushing in. I'd hurry over to close the shutters against the storm of awareness by loading up my tray with more commitments, obligations, and tasks. And then, I would binge.

The CEO of a top-shelf mastermind group geared to male entrepreneurs, Nate had come to me for help in scaling his enterprise to attract more clients without losing the intimacy and community he had curated. His goal was to double the size of his group and better target his offerings to keep participants highly engaged and active. He hired me to be a guest faculty member to teach his clients how to access their creativity and facilitate the establishment of a deeper, more robust feeling of safety in the group so that the members would find comfort in sharing things they might not share anywhere else.

"I've noticed there is a strong response every time you introduce concepts and exercises that help everyone tap into parts of themselves they didn't even know they had lost," Nate said. "I'm hearing anecdotes about increased problem-solving ability, access to ideas, even better sleep. The group is achieving more and doing less. They also seem to really be connecting with the work that requires vulnerability. Let's do more of that."

"I love hearing those results!" I said. "Of course, we can focus more on building creativity muscles and opening up through greater vulnerability. It might be worthwhile for you and me to do some work on this together, too, so that as you lead the group, you'll have—"

"Sorry, Susie. Someone's beeping in. I'll be right back."

There he goes. I waited a minute or two in silence.

"I'm back," he said. "Apologies. Where were we?"

If this had been a one-off occurrence, I would have thought nothing of it. There was a pattern, though, to how Nate took flight. I knew he genuinely wanted great results for the men in his mastermind group and was excited about the work we were doing together. I could see him begin to come alive in subtle ways. Tiny glimpses of the real Nate coming to the fore. He'd drop a poetic truth bomb in the group without even thinking, connecting immediately with everyone and setting off a forest fire of charged conversation. But just as the words left his lips, Nate would disappear again, leaving a void that confused the group. He'd return to operating out of his aloof, strategic mind, floating above our heads, putting distance between himself and the group.

"I was saying that it would be a good idea for you and me to do more of this work together," I said. "As we've discussed, I see real potential here for you to achieve scale if you commit to going through my entire coaching process."

"No doubt," he said. "So, when you are leading the group next week, I'd like..."

There he goes.

Underneath all that overdoing and hiding was a sensitive, observant soul with a heart of gold. By directing his attention outward to focusing solely on the group's experience, he had crafted a convenient, sanctioned way to duck away from doing his own work. This would function for a while. He could be superficial without losing engagement because of the raw power of his intellect and charisma. But without eventually doing the work himself, he was headed right for the Stagnation Zone, the land of diminished interest from his ideal clients—and dwindling revenue.

Each of us has our own work to do to get us to what we need to heal. Our resistance to change, to letting the emotions land, to opening up to being seen, is mighty. We become brilliantly skilled in building walls to avoid having to visit the patient who is part of us.

As we learned in chapter 2, The 5Ms are a weapon we can wield against this resistance, breaking apart our fortresses and enabling us to reclaim our creativity. The irony? We resist doing The 5Ms too. We stuff our "get out of jail free card" at the bottom of the deck.

Every morning when I sit for meditation, get out my laptop to write, get out my creativity supplies, or face a sixteen-ounce glass of fresh celery juice, it's a Groundhog Day of Inner Troll Battle.

I never feel like doing it. *Ever.*

It is a daily thought-sanitation project to do the work, maintain the healthy habit or ritual, and recommit to my goals.

Every damn day. I've come to expect the torrent of inner whining and whimpering and now am on high alert the minute my feet hit the floor. At that moment, the first opportunity to change my attachment to emotions that do not serve me presents itself.

It's a critical moment of choice. If I choose well, I launch a positive domino effect of momentum and more tiny wins. If I let the whiny thoughts have too much airtime, I get more and more creative as to why I am just not doing "X" today, justifying hiding out, staying small, and leaning into self-sabotage.

It is easy to let your ego show you a movie of the grand gestures it will take to accomplish grand goals. We can convince ourselves that we have to go from couch potato to scaling Mount Everest in two weeks, from doing little to no marketing work to spending five hours filling our sales pipelines, or from writer's block to a thousand words a day. Of course, we crave change. We may have plugged along in numbed-out denial for months and years in the Stagnation Zone. Once we decide to break free, though, we want to arrive. Be done.

This kind of grandiose, all-or-nothing thinking is just another snare set by our ego. We are oddly attracted to the ego's mental bullying, believing that if our effort is not enormous and immediate, we won't accomplish our goals.

That thinking is deeply flawed. Rather, it is the series of little steps, which compound over time, that take us where we want to go. This powerful progress is rooted in consistency and the law of accumulation. While our ego demands dramatic, fast results, magical alchemy begins with suiting up and taking small actions each day.

We are signaling to our brain that we are honoring a boundary we set for ourselves with love. Doing this each day builds a reservoir of confidence, well-being, and energy. It increases our desire to reach for other goals and make other good decisions.

We slowly slough off our old, small self and its small think-ing as we recommit to ourselves each day. With each little death, we become reborn, renewed, more alive. This death and rebirth process takes time. First, we have to loosen our-selves from the myths that promise grand results overnight. Lose twenty pounds in thirty days. Write a book in a week-end. Hit seven figures by the end of the quarter. Not only are such time frames wildly wrong and misleading, but they also miss the point. Sure, goals and achievements are magnificent. Once we reach them, however, we invariably find it doesn't feel as good as we thought it would. When I got out of debt and had financial freedom, of course, I was enormously relieved. Thrilled! But while I felt the release of the burden and stress, and a whooshing of joy and security, it didn't change how I felt in general or, most notably, how I felt about myself.

The incremental process, though, of becoming a new per-son through the breaking down and rebuilding of who I am brought me a calm that begins well before dawn and shad-ows me like a puppy all day. I maintain an equilibrium and the knowledge that I will prevail no matter what. Freedom! This keeps me willing to get back up each time I fall and skin my knees. Which happens *a lot*.

I know that we burn with the desire to get to the finish line. To stand in the frame of the "after" photo, all done with the journey. I also know that nothing I say right now will convince you that the gentle sloughing off of the old skin cells of you, the series of those tiny deaths, will end up being what you trea-sure most. You don't need to believe me yet. Please, though, observe yourself closely as you go about your transformation. Document it in your journal.

exercise Your "Before" and "After" Pictures

In detail, clearly describe your "before" picture. Where are you right now? Capture the metrics of how things stand. It could be your monthly revenue figures, how many days a week you exercise, your water intake, your current health numbers (blood sugar levels, blood pressure, weight, etc.), how many days a week you spend creating the new product or service you've dreamed of launching, how much time you spend with those you love, how much time you gift yourself play and rest.

Next, what do you want your "after" picture to look like? What are your new habits and rituals? Who is the desired future version of you? Get down all the details. What is frustrating you that you want to change? Write down all of those metrics. Focus, and resist the urge to do this exercise quickly. If you have trouble figuring out what you really want, start with writing down what you don't want any longer. All the things that are causing you pain. Then write down their opposite.

• • • • •

A word of caution. When you begin becoming the desired version of yourself, You 2.0, be aware that there may be people in your life who aren't excited that you are changing. They may feel threatened or frightened and want you to stay the "old" you. You may even encounter some odd attempts to throw you off your game, to keep you from establishing momentum for creating new habits, subtle or overt pressure to do the very things you want to stop doing.

I don't want you to be paranoid, just aware. Notice with curiosity how people react to your transformation. See who is genuinely excited and happy for you, who encourages you to keep going. And notice who tries to get you to stay the same or revert to the former version of you.

When Nate crossed the threshold and relented to doing the work himself, he struggled mightily at the onset. He wanted no part of this vulnerability business. His voice would crack and his confidence would falter as we hacked our way deeper into the jungle. During each session, he wanted to give up. Blow off the homework assignments.

As he witnessed what was happening in the mastermind group, though, he mustered up his own courage and returned to doing the work with me in one-on-one coaching sessions. With each lecture I gave in the group, his clients modeled for him what was possible—the strength, clarity, and calm that landed when hard-charging leaders were willing to break open and allow themselves to be seen.

A pivotal moment came the day Nate revealed to his clients where he had been resisting, hiding. He spoke of the work he was doing privately, releasing old habits and forming new daily rituals. He divulged how much energy he had been burning each day just to keep up the facade. When Nate let the walls come down and reconnected to himself, he channeled all of the resulting vitality into his creativity and his personal life. His work caught fire. He was enjoying a newfound passion for life he had not experienced since his youth. Nate had also begun rebuilding broken relationships with his wife and children and was devoting quality time to them each weekend. They had even booked a skiing trip for spring break.

The domino effects inside the mastermind group were immediate. Everyone seemed to exhale in unison and celebrate Nate. His willingness to share and make changes further reinforced his clients' commitments to doing the same. The bonds that formed in the group were profound and enduring.

Word got out about this powerhouse mastermind group that reshaped entrepreneurs, led by Nate, a formidable, relatable leader who could see and pull the greatness out of each participant because he could do the same for himself.

We can become the person who acts whether we feel like it or not. We can show up. Persevere. Keep the sacred promises to ourselves.

And as our becoming further unfolds, we create brand-new emotions, thinking, and realities as we embrace the world while standing in our infinite, innate power.

Letting Go

I've been a fan of all things nautical my entire life. Bodies of water, and the vessels for traversing them, give me a sense of unending potential for exploring and creating. The sailboat in particular captures my fascination, harnessing wind and waves to push through open water.

In the winter of 2016, I flew to Puerto Vallarta to take a weeklong keelboat certification course. Each day, we sailed out into the Bay of Banderas, and my instructor, Shawn, who looked like Ryan Reynolds with red hair, taught me each part of the boat, all the points of sail, and how to tack, jibe, perform water rescues, and dock. Each night, I'd read and study the manual, learning all the knots, sailing rights-of-way rules, and nautical terminology.

By the week's end, it was time to take the certification exam, both on the water and on paper. When I aced the exam, Shawn suggested we go out for a celebratory sail and bring along the spinnaker sail for extra fun.

Once out on the water, Shawn rigged up the spinnaker, which looks like half of a giant balloon, while I tended to the tiller, the lever on the back of the boat used for steering.

Shawn looked back over his shoulder and said, "Things are about to get really interesting!" I remained completely relaxed and confident, having no clue what he meant.

The moment the wind filled the spinnaker, the boat keeled over far to my right. I scrambled to get on the high side so I wouldn't fall out. I grabbed the tiller with a tight grip, trying to control what was happening. My brain shut down, flooded with fear.

Shawn looked back at me and yelled, "Stop trying to control the boat! You're gonna capsize us!"

I had no idea what to do.

"Loosen your grip on the tiller. Open your hand, and let it bob back and forth inside your hand. Feel these waves. The boat will tell you what it wants to do."

As a Class-A control freak, this ran counter to every instinct in my body. I knew if I didn't do exactly as he said, though, we would be in danger.

And so, because I had no choice, I let go. I 100 percent surrendered.

I felt the waves running beneath the boat, rising and swirling, pushing us this way and that. The tiller nudged me like a puppy to follow its lead. As soon as I let go, the boat responded. It felt like we were surfing on the wave tops, smooth and fast.

Shawn, with his back to me, yelled up at the sky, "You've got it!"

Up until that moment, I had only intellectually understood what surrendering meant. Now I knew what it felt like in my bone marrow. I now had muscle memory for how to stop directing, controlling, or demanding certain outcomes. The only way forward is to let the boat, or the situation, tell us what it wants to do.

I'm coming to understand just how much the ever-evolving "Now" wants us to relax our grip on our destinations. This doesn't mean sailing in circles without a charted course.

Rather, if we engage with our curiosity, agility, and creativity, we lead from our core, not our clipboard.

This builds authentic engagement and community among those in our organizations. And even more importantly, we begin to have the kind of crucial conversations that coax true innovation and new thinking to the fore.

When we let go of being rehearsed and scripted and are willing to trust ourselves, our actions and words connect.

Stephen Colbert, host of *The Late Show*, calls this connection with his audience "having emotional skegs in the water." He learned on election night in 2016 the powerful lesson of improvising and being authentic in the moment. Facing an audience in despair over the election results, Colbert decided to dig deep and go off script: "'The last ten minutes of that election show were honest. They were honest, and that was a turning point for us,' Colbert told *Variety*. 'After that, we knew I could never do the show without at least attempting to keep my emotional skegs in the water.' Each monologue he does now is 'an attempt to be honest with the audience so we can have an intimate relationship.'"

As entrepreneurs and creators, we often get stuck in our businesses and art. In those moments, when we don't know what to do and are reluctant to push through the uncertainty, we worry about making mistakes. Getting it wrong. But what if mistakes allow us to get better at our work? What if stepping forward where there is no road is the missing ingredient that ends up infusing us, and what we offer the world, with excitement, freedom, and untold possibility?

These are the very things our ideal market craves from us. Our prospective clients and buyers understand immediately if we have stepped out beyond the edge of our knowing. If we've done the work.

When the path disappears from beneath us, we begin using our intuition more. We start trying things we haven't tried before. Our true essence starts to show up. This energy is precisely what we want in our enterprises and in everything we create.

Incredible work comes from not knowing—the very thing we are trying to avoid. When we move in darkness, we mine the jewels of craft, creation, joy, and connection. This is the real conversation we want to have, and the one our ideal clients long for.

David Whyte reminds us that there are no courageous conversations without vulnerability. We will hold ourselves back, wall ourselves off, to keep pain out and our protection walls sturdy. And while our moat may keep barbs from reaching our flesh, the cost is a penetrating dullness and a lack of creativity:

> First of all, one of the powerful dynamics of leadership is being visible. One of the vulnerabilities of being visible is that when you're visible, you can be seen. And when you can be seen, you can be touched. And when you can be touched, you can be hurt.
>
> Some of us have these elaborate ways of looking as if we're showing up and not showing up. Except in an organizational setting, it has tremendous consequences on other people's lives. We've all worked in organizations where someone is sitting there at a crossroads or nexus in the organization. They're there, but they're not there. And because of that, they're blocking everything that's trying to come through their particular portal. So one of the dynamics you have to get over with is this idea that you can occupy a position of responsibility, that you can have a courageous conversation without being vulnerable.

Our customers, readers, followers, audience members, colleagues, and children know when our oars are resting in our lap—or as Stephen Colbert would say, when our emotional skegs are not in the water. When we are not invested. Not visible. Not vulnerable. When we are playing it safe and sticking to a script, it's so easy to tune us out.

But when our oars are deep in the emotional current, reverberating with passion from a deeply vulnerable place inside of us, the world will stand still, sit up, and hang on our every word.

Can you spot where your oars are resting in your lap in your business and personal life? Where are you holding back? Where are you unwilling to be vulnerable?

As wildly uncomfortable as it is for me, embracing not knowing and releasing prescribed agendas connects me to the best version of myself and opens doors to synchronicity. It signals a playful energy to the Universe, too, which answers our courage and openness with magic made manifest.

exercise Letting Go (With Watercolors)

Go to your local discount store and select an inexpensive set of watercolor paints, a watercolor brush or two, and a pad of watercolor paper. Don't fret over the colors, brands, or sizes of the brushes. Cut out nine three-by-three-inch squares from your watercolor paper. With a pencil, draw a circle inside each of the nine squares.

Fill a plastic cup with water and place a paper towel or two near you. Open your paints and dip your brush into the water. Select a color and swirl your brush inside it. Take your loaded brush and begin plopping color onto one of your circles. Completely cover the circle with paint. Rinse your brush in the water and then select another color. Bring your brush over to your still-wet circle and begin dabbing color a little bit at a time onto the surface. Notice how the wet paint is uncontrollable, how it runs. The first time we witness how watercolor wants to behave, it can fill us with an odd combination of delight and frustration.

Continue painting each of your circles and dabbing in different colors. As you experiment and try novel color combinations and varying amounts of water, most likely you'll find some of the results positively gorgeous. Some not so much. The results, the circles you paint, are immaterial. Cut out your circles and paste them in your journal.

This is an opportunity to let yourself loosen your grip on the tiller of you and the world and notice how that feels. Letting go can let in more daylight, empower us to take on bigger risks, and settle us into our imagination.

The Power of the Unscripted Self

I stood in front of my fellow Transformational Speaking Immersion students in a suite in Santa Fe's Las Palomas hotel and began to tell my story.

When I was three or so sentences in, Real Speaking founder Gail Larsen looked up from her notes and interrupted me. "You're too cerebral," she said. "Stop thinking and scripting your story. Connect back to your HomeZone and speak from your heart. Trust the words will come."

In other words, "Get out of your head and into your truth." I started again. I got a bit further into my story before I ran back to the barn of safety by leaning into my brain for language. Gail stopped me again. This time, she pointed out where I had made an impromptu action with my journal to illustrate a part of my story, and said how much it had resonated with her: "I'm on that beach with you when you drop your journal. Speak from that place."

I kept telling myself, "Get out of your head," but it wasn't that easy. I bumbled my way through my story, falling in and out of my need to control a presentation rather than share a deeply felt experience. It was such a relief to finally arrive at the end and sit down, out of Gail's scrutiny.

The part of me I had always relied on, my intellect, was now my biggest stumbling block. No matter how insecure I felt, I always knew I could double down on studying more, pushing my strategic brain to find the right answers and ace the test. Excel at any task. Now, that part of me was of no use on the battlefield of vulnerability. My power drained and faded, and my over-achiever heart sank.

Heat rose in my chest, upward to my face and ears. It turned out that the woman who aced a public speaking course in college couldn't speak her way out of a paper bag. My mind turned gelatinous with shame.

We worked intensely for four days, connecting with and deeply dropping into the truest and most vulnerable parts of ourselves. We uncovered what it is about us that is unique. It was an exhausting and profoundly powerful experience.

When I boarded my return flight in Albuquerque, I knew something in me had shifted forever, and that I possessed the keys to connecting with and moving others through story, whether in speaking or writing.

My challenge would be to stay there, in that place of trust and surrender, far from the briar patch of my controlling, analytical mind.

As entrepreneurs and creators, we succeed by connecting with our ideal clients and moving them to action. Whether we are marketing a product, firing up our audience to act, or coaching clients to become the best versions of themselves, absolutely everything rides on how well we connect through story. To do this, you have to learn to get out of your head and into your truth.

"If you want to change the world, tell a better story."

Gail Larsen

Our stories and images hold magic. By sharing them within our campfire communities, we can teach and reach and effect change. Your ideal clients can feel when you drop into the core of who you truly are. When you trust your voice. It will take on a cello-like, warm, alluring tone when you are there—or sound jagged like permafrost spikes when you are out of sync, dog-paddling in currents of control.

Going off script and trusting the power of our stories teaches us that surrender connects beyond words and reaches the heart in powerful and indelible ways.

exercise The Wild You

Who are you in the wild? The unfettered you? Can you come up with one word that describes who you are when you are without restriction, without bounds?

Take out your journal and write that word in the middle of the page. Bring to mind four to six colors that fill you with an energy you love, that represent the way your "wild" one-word description of you makes you feel. Next, either print out or paint solid sheets of those colors or purchase a pad of construction paper containing your colors.

Without thinking, begin cutting shapes out of your sheets of color. You can cut out primary shapes, little coils, wavy strands, shapes of animals you love, stars, symbols, etc. Just let go and cut out a variety of different-sized shapes.

Bringing your focus now to the "wild you," begin selecting shapes from your pile and pasting them around your word. Focus not on making "art," but rather on capturing an accurate representation of the unbound you. You without limits.

What does your unscripted self look like? How do you act? What kind of energy do you emanate into the world? Try to capture those answers in your shapes as you design the page of your wild self.

Seeing and Being Seen
. . . .

"It's luminous, it's uplifting, it has many layers, but it always comes back to being present, breathing, maintaining eye contact."
HOW ONE VISITOR DESCRIBED SITTING WITH ARTIST
MARINA ABRAMOVIĆ

In 2010 at the Museum of Modern Art (MoMA), Marina Abramović engaged in an extended performance called *The Artist Is Present*. More than 750,000 people stood in line for the chance to sit across from her and communicate with her nonverbally.

The MoMA website explains, "Over the course of nearly three months, for eight hours a day, [Abramović] met the gaze of 1,000 strangers, many of whom were moved to tears."

Abramović said that "'Nobody could imagine ... that anybody would take the time to sit and just engage in a mutual gaze with me'... In fact, the chair was always occupied, and there were continuous lines of people waiting to sit in it. 'It was [a] complete surprise ... this enormous need of humans to actually have contact.'"

As much as we crave being truly seen and connecting deeply with others, we can also scurry out of that light like a cockroach. We have a "push me, pull you" relationship with visibility's double-edged sword. One side is empowerment, affirmation, and soulful belonging. The other is the risk and fear of harsh judgment.

We tend to be uncomfortable at first with such focused attention. Then there comes a moment, the moment of letting go and settling in, when we transcend the fear. Release our death grip on the tiller and begin to trust.

And how do we do this seemingly impossible thing of letting go and trusting? If you are like me, there may always be vestigial remains of the fear of risking exposure. If that is the case, here's the good news: We can overcome it. We start the process of letting others see us when *we let ourselves see us*. And how do we begin to truly see ourselves? When we are immersed in what we love to do.

How is it that we became so separated from ourselves? It began when we gave up the activities that let us express the very depths of our souls. That is, when we were active, but most likely unknowing, accomplices in letting parts of us die.

That death is not simply the absence of creative expression. The withered part of our souls does not lie dormant. Rather, it becomes toxic and metastasizes, devouring well-being and the delicious sense of being seen and heard and replacing it with repressed, tightly corked energy that rots and eventually pushes to the fore as anxiety.

This is not a simple "use it or lose it" parable. This is much stronger: use it or suffer.

exercise Reconnecting with Your Playful Heart

Reflect on the kinds of creative pursuits you once had. Include all of the ways you used to engage in imaginative play. What were you doing? Where were you? Were you alone, or, if in company, who was with you? Write it all down in your journal.

Next, have a look at your play history work from chapter 4. When you compare your answers to the questions above with your play histories, what do you notice? What patterns do you see?

Understanding all the things that used to bring us joy is a key step in turning things around. We cannot shift our behavior if we do not have all the intel. This is not trivial work. This is central to building creative confidence. The pursuits that bring us happiness are myelin sheaths for our jagged, exposed, vulnerable nerve endings. Soothing, calming, stirring. Play takes us up and over the hurdles, releasing and infusing us with energy.

Now that you have written down all the activities that lift your spirits and free your mind, let's *do* them. The results do not need to be complicated, expensive, or Instagram-worthy! Decide what you want to reconnect with and go off and indulge. Every couple of weeks at a minimum (notice I did not say each quarter or each year!), schedule a mini, joyful adventure that takes you right to your Joy Sources.

When I first began reconnecting with my playful heart, these sojourns into fun (inspired by author Julia Cameron's Artist Dates) were sweet dew on parched earth. I took day trips to bookstores, art supply stores, movie theaters, art galleries, lectures, readings, plays, and concerts. I'd take longer excursions to farther destinations, luxuriate in getting lost on purpose in unfamiliar places, and take art and culinary classes. Like a desert after a soaking rain, color began blooming in all areas of my life.

I began attracting the support and resources I needed to expand my business. I made decisions with ease and speed, which propelled results. I shook off mistakes and snags and refused to stay stuck. If something really went off the rails, I gifted myself the ability to feel sorry for myself for about eight hours, and then it was right back on that pony.

I got my sense of humor back. People started commenting on how funny I was. I stopped being so serious all the time, acting as if the world's fate was my responsibility. Higher-end deals showed up, as did clients who not only intuited my coaching was a perfect fit for what they needed, but also valued my expertise and time.

Play both energizes us and settles our minds. It helps seed our thoughts with more positive "what if?" thinking. We begin trying more and more daring pursuits with relaxed shoulders, open to chance encounters and synchronicities.

Finding and speaking with our authentic voice is essential to being fully alive, connected, and creative. Revealing who we truly are, what we believe and value, and even what keeps us up at night can be very scary business. Allowing ourselves to be fully seen risks rejection, ridicule, and shame.

Stepping fully into our voice, therefore, requires complete vulnerability. As Brené Brown notes, vulnerability is a two-sided coin: "vulnerability is the core of shame and fear and our struggle for worthiness, but it appears that it's also the birthplace of joy, of creativity, of belonging, of love." If we want to experience the thrill and satisfaction of connection, we must have the courage to be imperfect while being immensely kind and compassionate with ourselves.

In all the hustle of the everyday chase, we forget that the offering the world holds most dear is us. Our unvarnished, open selves. Aware, awake, tuned in, and willing to truly connect.

Remember: We start the process of letting others see us when *we let ourselves see us*. And how do we begin to truly see ourselves? When we are immersed in what we love to do.

That gnawing knowing inside of you is telling you something. Your racing pulse and anxious mind are signs that it's time to course-correct. Happily, your playful heart and creativity are right where you left them, months or years ago. Saunter over and reintroduce yourself.

The Thing Keeping You from Your Greatness

· · · · · · · · · · · · · · · · · · · ·

I could tell the minute I got into the pool that the 6:00 a.m. swimmers were an entirely different breed from the 7:00 a.m. swimmers. These folks were not messing around. Focused and fierce. Each lane contained a proficient swimmer, powering through the water like a goggles-wearing dolphin. That level of athleticism is a thing of inspirational beauty.

A fellow in the center lane motioned me over. "You don't have to wait for an open lane. Come on in my lane, I'll be finishing up in about ten minutes. You can have this side."

Delighted by his generosity, I joined his lane and started swimming. A moment or two later, he powered by my side, cutting through the water like a hot knife in a stick of butter. It was one thing to see him swim from a distance, quite another to be right next to him.

"Wow," I said softly through exhaled bubbles. "Michael Phelps Jr."

A couple of weeks later, I saw him again. We took a moment to chat at the deep end of the pool while we caught our breath. He said that when he had first started swimming a few years ago, he could barely get halfway across the pool.

"The first few times I did it, I started choking and gagging," he said with a laugh. "I thought I was gonna die."

I stared at him and shook my head while treading water. "That can't be. I mean, you are one of the best swimmers I have ever seen."

"Yep, nearly drowned my first few times." He went on to explain he was training to compete in a triathlon world championship.

As many times as I have learned this lesson, this time it truly landed: few of us are born with a golden skill set—most often, we fail and flail our way to greatness.

"Vulnerability is not weakness; it's our greatest measure of courage."

Brené Brown

The champions in life, business, and art are simply the ones who started out with a willingness to get it all wrong. To look like a complete idiot. To join in and not care if they were picked last.

exercise Your Wildest Dream

Take a minute now and think of the thing you really want to do. Your biggest, wildest, most improbable dream. Don't censor yourself. Let the ideas you have been carrying and burying for months or years rise up in your conscious mind.

See it clearly. Write it all down in your journal.

* * * * *

When we have visions of pursuing the things that call our heart, they tend to be quickly followed by doomsday images generated by our inner critic. One minute we are living out the dreamy images in our minds. The next, we are watching a reel of our spectacular failures and hideously public flame-outs.

Maybe, we reason, we are not ready. Maybe, we console ourselves, it is best to stick with what we know. Maybe, we say while floating in a sea of denial, we don't really want to do that thing after all.

Here's my theory: the happiest, most creatively expressive, most fulfilled, most successful people are simply those who are willing to drive their metaphorical cars right into a ditch.

When I launched my real estate business during the height of the Great Recession, I took a deep breath and placed what little money I had all on the equivalent of 37 black on the roulette table. I did not know if I had enough runway to get the plane of my enterprise into the air before my money ran out. I was willing to find out, though. And I was willing for it all to collapse. I figured it really could not get much worse than where I was, financially and otherwise.

The audaciousness required to start a company in such precarious conditions uncorked a raw and edgy adventurousness that made me an idea magnet. The moment I took one step forward onto that invisible path, not knowing if there would be anything beneath my feet, the creativity angels swarmed around me. They stayed right by my side for the entire time I owned the firm, through the day I sold it to my hand-picked successors.

Please note: If you are in a precarious financial position, I am not advocating that you take giant risks, burn the boats, and proceed without capping your downside. By the time I launched my real estate firm, I had ten years of experience in the industry and a proven track record of success. Yes, I was building the plane while I flew it in very turbulent weather, but I was also a seasoned and savvy pilot.

MY CLIENT Richard had an on-brand, silly idea for a new product launch. While most of his competitors chose to associate with elite imagery and messaging, Richard went all in on humor, kindness, and problem solving. He zagged and darted away from the entire school of competitor fish, who ended up looking like an amorphous blob of sameness to the consumer. Richard was willing to make fun of himself while still holding on to his positioning as a respected thought leader (quite a feat). He did worry that the campaign would fall flat on its face, but he pressed forward and launched his new product. The market ate his schtick right up and proceeded to completely ignore his competitors, rewarding him with top market share for months.

Richard stopped worrying about what others thought about him and took a creative leap. He was willing to sit in uncomfortable uncertainty while enjoying the freedom of playfulness with his marketing. Not only did his courage pay dividends in sales, but also he was able to attribute his enduring, sticky messaging to the emotions evoked in his ideal customers. By connecting them with his daring exuberance, he helped unleash these very same emotions in those who purchased from him again and again.

The fascinating thing about learning to fly is that once you let yourself stand on the edge of the nest, flap your wings with determination, and still hit the ground, you find the humor in it all. You learn how to observe yourself with just enough distance to not take yourself too seriously.

The trying, the doing, seems to release a chemical in our brains that bolsters our sense of self, our courage reserves. We approach the next scary thing more readily. We spend less and less time pacing back and forth on the diving board, mustering up the bravery to jump.

What can you do today that has a bit of thorny reputational risk to it, even if that risk is to your own opinion of yourself? You can and will figure it out. Make it a game.

Confidence follows willingness, not the other way around. Be willing to take a wrong turn. Burn the sauce. Paint something hideous. Launch a dud of a marketing campaign. Get it all wrong. Break your own heart.

Free yourself from yourself.

exercise Writing a Poem

Continuing with our theme of embracing our journal as our place to practice, explore, and take risks, let's try our hand at writing a short poem.

Yes, a poem. Trust me, you are about to completely surprise yourself!

Bring a story to mind. Something moving, tragic, or jubilant. A true story. The key is that this story did not happen to you, but rather someone close to you. Have the story?

Next, set a timer for ten minutes. In your journal, write a poem about this thing that happened *as if it had happened to you.* Do not fret over rhyming words or meter or standard poem punctuation. Just reach into your subconscious, retrieve the emotion, and share it on the page.

When the timer goes off, stop. Take a look at your last line and spend a minute or so wrapping it up. Next, read your poem aloud, slowly. Let the warmth of your words and the sounds from your throat hang in the air all around you. Pause at the end and close your eyes.

Notice what is happening inside your body, the vibration.

The new sense of freedom.

On the page opposite your poem, answer this: What is it that would make all the difference for me right now? What feels too scary to try that I've longed to do? Spend five minutes writing your answer.

inspiration beacon

FIND A recording of a poet reading their work aloud. YouTube is a great place to stumble across works you may never have heard before. Before your next walk, play the clip and listen intently. Take the poem in your mind and heart as you walk. Let it sit inside you, undisturbed.

The Only Way Out Is Through

"Don't wish it were easier. Wish you were better."
JIM ROHN

In the late spring of 1974, Steven Spielberg had a problem. More accurately, he had several problems. He was about to begin filming the movie *Jaws*, without a script, without a cast, and without a shark.

Spielberg pushed forward anyway with determination, spirit, and courage. He and the writers worked on the script the night before each day of filming, and many times, they decided with cast members what would go into the movie. As a result, many rich improvisations found their way into the film.

The mechanical shark, Bruce, constantly malfunctioned. They dealt with numerous challenges that filming at sea presented: waning light, seasick crew members, and boats sailing into view during shooting. The project ran way over budget, and Spielberg and many of the actors feared their careers were over.

Yet, they all pressed forward. It was a harrowing 159 days of filming. Each day was a test of endurance, creativity, and innovative thinking. The constraints they dealt with, such as not having their main character functioning for most of the filming, forced one of the most creative and thrilling aspects of the film.

For instance, the horizontal waterline shots, where we saw legs underneath the water and bodies above the water, added to our sense of impending doom, heightening our perspective of the vulnerability of the swimmers. Our not being able to see the shark turned out to be exponentially more terrifying. The iconic music denoting the approaching shark filled our minds with frightening images we created, far exceeding the power of having the image shown to us.

If the experience of the filmmakers and actors had been less challenging, I believe the end result would not have been the same blockbuster movie that thrilled and captivated millions of viewers, scaring some so much that they never went into the ocean again.

Spielberg spent his 159 days of filming being tested, stretched, and pulled from every angle. His experience is a powerful lesson for all of us. The times we are most tested are not fun to live through, as the process of being dissolved and reshaped can be painful. But they are often the best levers for our creativity.

Every one of us experiences such trials and tribulations when we are creating something. This is simply part of the process. The difficulty, the challenge, the uncomfortable remaking of who we are is the point. Sometimes, many times, even more so than the end result of what we are making.

I have begun experimenting with an entirely new mindset when I am up to my knees in a creative project. Rather than sitting in the dark ready to cover my eyes with my hands when the scary stuff shows up, I walk right toward it.

Yes, it is going to hurt. The work will be hard. But I know the best part of me will show up as a result. The most layered and creative version of me will crawl from her shell with claws at the ready.

We've got to hack our way through the jungle while simultaneously forging the machete we need for the job. The tool we need will reveal itself to us. Let yourself not know throughout the entire process, because that's how the magic shows up. The troubles we encounter along the way make our work, and us, better. Note: This is not my favorite thing! No matter how many times I have walked into the unknown, I still want to try to control how things will go. But we cannot. The only way out is through surrendering and doing the work. This is your own personal jungle, and no one else can clear the way.

The fear of the unknown may be a well-disguised version of the fear of being who we truly are. It may be easier to not boldly be ourselves. Not show what we see. Not reveal our vision of the world and her inhabitants and reflect that back in our art. It is always easier to stall. Water down the expressive parts of us. Not ruffle feathers. If we don't move, there won't be any ripples in the water. If we don't breathe, maybe no one will even know we are here.

Show up anyway. Move and breathe and create.

It's going be hard. Harder than we ever imagined. The challenge is the fire that takes the glass of us and shapes us into a new form with dazzling colors. The choice, then, is to show all of our colors or die on the vine comfortable. Let's say who we are and mean it.

Don't pray for mythical gifts or talents; pray for perseverance and the ability to exhale deeply and dive in. The gifts will arrive in the doing, during your time in the fire. The flames will take you further forward in your provenance of becoming, where you will find at last the freedom and enduring impact you seek.

exercise Focusing Your Perspective

Take a four-by-six-inch index card and cut a one-inch square in the center. This square hole is going to be your viewfinder on a photography field trip. Go on a short stroll, taking your phone and your index card. As you walk, notice what grabs your attention. When something has stopped you, take your index card and place it in varying positions and angles over the object of interest. How does moving the viewfinder change the object and your perspective of it?

When you find something compelling inside your viewfinder, snap a picture of it. Continue walking, noticing, framing the things around you, and photographing them. Once home, print out the images, cut them out, and paste them in your journal.

Do you see a pattern of the things that caught your eye and how you framed them? Did you discover unexpected beauty as you photographed everyday things? How did your perspective and powers of noticing shift as you moved along?

The Artist
and the
Entrepreneur

"In order to lead others, we have to know how to find our own way."

MARTHA BECK

I WAS SIXTEEN YEARS OLD and in heaven.

I was perched in the summer sun on the steps leading to the back of my dad's shop. I had a small radio playing Top 40 hits by my side. I was on my first *usubata*, a Japanese vase, carefully rubbing away dirt and grime with a copper penny, painstakingly revealing a beautiful, patinaed bronze surface.

This would be the only piece I would finish for the day. I'd work on and complete another the next day. And another the next. By summer's end, the entire crate of pieces that had spent weeks on a ship from Japan would shimmer and shine on the shelves of my dad's shop, alongside other ikebana vases, books, shears, and *kenzan* (the spiky "frogs" used to position flowers in ikebana containers).

At the dinner table each night, we'd laugh and say it was my summer of Japanese bronze. Eight hours a day, six days a week, from June to August. Copper and bronze.

What special magic did my dad possess to get a teenager to do such work for an entire summer with a happy heart? It started with his passion for exquisite objects, birthed by Asian artisans he deeply admired, and his ongoing quest to search out and bring them to the mountains of North Carolina.

Rewind to the spring day we stood on the grassy hill behind his shop, The Stone Lantern, broke away the metal bands from a wooden crate with a crowbar, and lifted the lid.

I stood next to my dad as he sank his hands into the white straw with the excitement of a child on Christmas morning and lifted out the first *usubata*. He gently, lovingly, wiped away the straw and dust, stopping to take in the craftsmanship. I watched him closely, and in that moment, I learned how reverence and deep appreciation look on a face.

"Probably sixteenth century," he said, holding the piece up for me to see. "Look at the detail here. Think of the patience, passion, and devotion it took to make this."

I kept my gaze on Dad as he turned the *usubata* in the sun, admiring each inch. I thought of the artist, hundreds of years earlier, caring for their every move as they worked the bronze into life. The four of us—the artist, my dad, the *usubata*, and me—were now forever connected across space and time.

Dad showed me how to gently remove the layers of gunk that coated the surface. "You can use a penny... copper is softer than bronze and won't scratch it. See? As you move the penny across, little by little, you can give this piece new life, showing its full beauty."

I was all in. This was not "grunt work." This was a mission on Beauty's behalf. An homage to the artist across centuries and miles. A desire to share with the world the tingly sensation in my stomach and heart when in the presence of passion, creation, and exquisite design.

In other summers, I'd witness my dad crawl inside the display windows to extract dead bugs. I'd watch him wash the sink in the flower studio with his bare hands. I'd overhear him delight customers with the history, culture, and artful practices of Japan.

I'd stand next to him out front and help check out customers as they brought their treasures to the counter. I'd learn how to do things "the Stone Lantern way," with a fierce attention to detail, love, and care. And on the rare occasions we made a mistake, I watched him handle and resolve customer complaints with gentleness and grace, ensuring each was not just satisfied, but also overwhelmed with surprise and gratitude.

Dad embodied what it means to place yourself in a business and life you love. He led by ensuring he was immersed in beauty, art, and discovery, the very things that brought him alive. He led by example. He never asked us to do work he wasn't willing to do himself with a happy spirit. We couldn't help but want to work with him and do whatever we could to support him and the shop. We, too, brought our best selves to each task.

Dad knew what called to his heart, and he never let naysayers talk him out of what brought him joy. When he announced he was opening an Asian art gallery in 1960 in Highlands, a tiny, remote town in the mountains, everyone thought he was insane. How could he sustain himself in a town of 1,500 residents and several thousand summer visitors?

Why did he choose Highlands? Because Dad thought the verdant, ancient mountains ringed in mist were an idyllic setting. Highlands was also a resort town, and he knew that sophisticated collectors from the Southeast would visit the cool mountains in the summer to escape the heat. He knew beauty's transformational powers and spent his days bringing that alchemy to the lives of his customers through his stunning ikebana arrangements and assortment of antiques, porcelains, artworks, and collectibles. It turned out to be a wise bet.

The Stone Lantern was nearly everyone's favorite stop in Highlands from 1960 until the day my dad died in 2015. It was an oasis on Main Street that transported you from everyday life to a realm of magic, culture, and devotion to the artist's sublime gifts.

Dad also did the hard work on himself before seeking to build his enterprise. He spent years educating and testing himself, and crafting an unparalleled self-awareness through self-leadership. All across Asia, he found his way, without maps or guides, building relationships with vendors, selecting merchandise, and creating a detailed vision for his shop and brand.

As entrepreneurs and creators leading businesses, we often forget the importance of doing self-discovery before we seek to build the ultimate team and attract clients. We'd rather fast-forward over that uncomfortable patch of work and time. It's easier to focus on helping others than to focus inward.

Skipping our own wayfinding, though, short-circuits our connection with ourselves and, in turn, with our ideal clients. Not only do we miss crucial clues for how to pull our clients into our orbit with ease, but also we are at sea energetically. Those we want to reach the most will not pick up on, or resonate with, our signals.

Be willing to heal the broken places in your heart and eliminate the habits that do not serve you. Let yourself get lost on purpose as you voyage over dark seas with only stars to guide you. Invest mightily in your growth, development, mindset, and self-awareness. It is only then that you can lead through how you show up in the world.

We know if you've done the work. We can feel your energy before you speak or write. We can already see your heart. We want to follow those who lead by example, who are a few steps down the path from us and continue to be on the journey, always willing to do the hard work on themselves first. Let us follow your model, your example. Show us what you have healed, what you have transmuted, what you love, and what remains unresolved. Show us what reverence and deep appreciation look like on your face.

inspiration beacon

LET'S MAKE a yummy puttanesca sauce—delicious and very easy!

YOU'LL NEED

3-4 Tbsp olive oil

1 small onion, diced

1 Tbsp of anchovy paste (optional)

4 or more cloves garlic, finely chopped

Red pepper flakes, to taste

1 ½ 28-oz cans whole plum tomatoes

Freshly ground black pepper and salt, to taste

1 can of artichoke hearts

1 cup of pitted black olives

2 Tbsp capers

Fresh parsley and oregano, chopped

1 package of your preferred pasta

Fresh basil leaves, shredded

Shaved Parmesan cheese

INSTRUCTIONS

Bring a pot of salty water to boil.

Warm 3 Tbsp of olive oil with the diced onion and anchovy paste in a large skillet over medium-low heat. Cook, stirring occasionally, until the onion is translucent, about 8 minutes. Add in the garlic and pepper flakes and cook for just a minute (don't let it burn).

Drain the tomatoes and crush them into chunks. Add them to the skillet, with some salt and pepper. Raise the heat to medium-high and cook, stirring occasionally, for about 10 minutes. Stir in the artichoke hearts, olives, capers, and continue to simmer. Add in the parsley and oregano.

Cook the pasta, stirring occasionally, until it is al dente (follow package instructions). Drain quickly, reserving one cup of water. Add ¼–½ cup of pasta water (to your desired consistency) to the sauce along with the remaining olive oil and basil. Toss the pasta into the sauce. Plate immediately and sprinkle shaved Parmesan cheese on top, if desired.

Enjoy!

Your Business (Art) Is a Mirror

"You use a glass mirror to see your face; you use works of art to see your soul."
GEORGE BERNARD SHAW

I am working with two entrepreneur clients who share many things in common: fierce intelligence, a servant leader's heart, a willingness to work incredibly hard, and a true mastery of their craft.

Jamie is unapologetically, and kindly, herself. She continues to out herself and reveal where she is scared, resistant to change, frustrated, overwhelmed, and fearful when facing uncertainty. She will also boldly declare what and whom she loves, what lights her up, what resonates with her, and what profoundly inspires her.

I can easily see the art of who she is. Her expressive vulnerability is a breath of fresh air. I often experience an electric range of emotions when talking with her. It is an adventure to go on a conversational ride together. Up, down, sideways, and inside out, she gives me the full and raw experience of what it means to be her.

Another client, Kim, has perfected a series of filters through which she screens every thought, idea, comment, business move, and decision. In any moment, she could choose her family filter, her appeasing filter, her pleasing filter, her upbringing filter, or her control filter. She expends vast amounts of energy each day second-guessing her innate wisdom and intuition and trying to figure out what she thinks the world wants from her.

Over many months, I have helped her excavate her true self, pebble by pebble, and see the full range and brilliance of who she is, unplugged. When I describe certain aspects and qualities of her aloud, she reacts with surprise and delight at being truly seen. Her giddiness quickly fades, though, into a mix of horror and shock that a piece of the greater puzzle of her is now exposed in the wild. She quickly lowers the curtain on her self-expression. She gets antsy and tries to rein in how much of her I can see.

Guess which one of these entrepreneurs is rocketing toward the stratosphere in her business? Which one readily connects with clients, drawing them to her like honeybees wanting to sit upon the bold colors of her petals?

Which one gets to the end of a pitch with warmth and humor, feeling as if she has won the business, only to find out the client rarely buys or commits? Which one must continually replenish her business pipeline because clients disengage and drop out of her membership program after a few weeks?

We entrepreneurs and creators make the same mistake, over and over: we forget that our best marketing elixir and magic maker is *us*. The unvarnished, unfiltered us. We forget that our creative self-expression and our businesses at their best and worst—our art—are mirrors of who and how we are— the many ways we choose to fill our hearts and souls with song, poetry, and beauty; the time we offer our ragged bodies to rest and recover; the gentle yet firm boundaries we keep to protect our sacred energy; the quiet in which we can hear ourselves think and remember what we have forgotten or pushed aside; the time we spend moving our bodies or making something.

You can smile at me through tired eyes that do not lift and crinkle, and I will not trust you or believe you are happy or sincere. You can talk fast and push bonuses and deadlines to entice me to sign up, and I will not give you my credit card number. You can hustle and holler, but if who you are and what you are saying are hollow or do not ring true, I will walk on.

In the same way, your creativity, your unique, competitive edge, will get up and go too. It's not because we can't afford it or aren't interested that we are not buying from you. We are not buying from you because we cannot *see* you. The real you. Your art. Who you are is what you create. And it is in that reflection that we fall in love with your art as you.

We entrepreneurs can believe only in business mechanics, amping our platforms, and finding productivity hacks. But our time and attention are much better spent in discovering the center of our broken hearts and showing *that* to the world.

And when we forget who we truly are, we feel the nauseating awareness of having made it while lying to ourselves. Somewhere buried in our subconscious, we know we are on borrowed time, and that the ghost of our true self will soon come calling, bill in hand.

When there is a disconnect between our energy and what or who we want to engage with, our efforts will fall flat. We can furrow our brows and white-knuckle an effort all we want, and all our toiling will be to no avail. Our energy always, always precedes us and our desired outcomes.

I am reminded of this every time I invite creativity to engage with me. If I am in a funk, or believing a painful thought to be true, creativity will scamper off behind the bushes, out of sight and reach. Our emotions are frequencies that vibrate throughout the core of our being. If I am in martyr mode, feeling sorry for myself and believing the task in hand is too hard, too overwhelming, creativity will simply answer with, "Agree."

But when I am confident, playful, energetic, and clear, creativity will cozy up to me without even being called. I find myself in a delicious state of flow, bending time as ideas and execution roll right along on their own power, like a marble on a slanted table.

Creativity thrives in curiosity, authenticity, experimentation, wonder, and play. If you are hitting a wall, stuck, let that be a sign that you haven't found the channel yet, and need to adjust.

In such moments, we can take a brief inventory by asking ourselves some questions:

- What is it that we believe to be true? Have we bought the lie that we are not up to the task?

- What is it that we need right now? Do we need an accountability buddy? A coach to help us blast through our outer shells of concrete? A trusted council of entrepreneurs to help us process ideas or get clarity? Time, or rest, or singular focus? Fresh air? A snack?

- And a biggie: Are we in create mode or imitate mode? Are we working from a place that is in complete alignment with our essential nature, or are we copying what others

"Imagination is therefore
the most potent
force in the universe . . .
It's the one skill in life that
benefits from ignoring
what everyone else knows."

Kevin Kelly

are doing because we lack the confidence in our own ideas or are following the advice of "an expert" who said that's what we should do?

As we dance with creativity, let's check in first and ask if it feels like freedom and truth. Does the work open you up, or is it closing you off from yourself and your desired audience like a mean rumor hissed into your ear?

Like the birds that sing right before dawn, we can call out from our perches and receive a call back from creativity that forms a melody, our unique song. It will resonate throughout the woods and lift the hearts of those still in darkness searching for their own music.

When we step into our own river of desire, we find the raw material for our creative voice and vision. We follow the butterfly that catches our eye and brings it to light.

The water swirling around our ankles is our river and ours alone. If we want the ecstasy of true connection and resonance within and without, we first must know the water that comprises us. From there, we drink with cupped hands and delight in the quenching of a thirst we did not know we had.

Ignoring What Everyone Else Knows

As David spoke, the image in my mind was of him floating high above his body, staring down in judgment, fierce and unrelenting. Pain hung onto his heart like fat waterdrops on leaves after a spring rain.

"I watch them, you know," he said. "The seven-figure entrepreneurs. How they are running their businesses. What kind of lifestyles they have."

"Yeah?" I asked. "What is it exactly that comprises the gap between where they are and where you are? Let's break it down."

I already knew the answers. I waited to hear the words echo from the phone speaker. The over-the-shoulder view of someone with a core belief that who he is, what he values, what he loves, what he dreams of, and how he has chosen to build his business and life are somehow not right. Off. Not enough. I'd hear that he feels inept. That he's not doing the right things, not focused on the right audience. His life is dull and lackluster in comparison.

David is a brilliant coach for artists who have lost their connection with their desire to make art. Artists who no longer approach their work with joy and passion, but instead are filled with dread, avoiding their studios and canvases. He has created stunning and impactful content that most of those "seven-figure entrepreneurs" would give their right arms to have. He has organically grown his list and has a majority of repeat business and strong referral deal flow. Clients trust him. They surrender to him.

David has a way of helping his clients reach within and discover the buoyant fingerprint of their souls. He is the perfect sherpa through hellfire because he has lived and survived it. And he is determined to let other wayward travelers in on the secrets. The kicker is that from any vantage point, his business and life are carpeted in the greenest of grass.

How do we dislodge ourselves from the claustrophobic squeeze of the boulders on either side of our shoulders? How do we wriggle out of stuckness, out of the mire of the mind swamp, and shake off the debris of our painful, habitual thinking?

We can start by imagining what freedom feels like. Looks like. Sounds like. We can imagine the old worries evaporating. What would that require? What would we have to change, begin, or stop doing?

We can imagine the return of our happy-go-lucky, adventurous soul. Where is it and what is it doing? To whom does it want to be a hero? We can imagine the ideal day we want to live. Our ideal clients. Our ideal vision of how we'd serve and how often.

Is there a yearlong sabbatical calling you? Maybe spent living overseas or traveling? Is your vision a high-volume enterprise with an expansive team or a tight ship, lean and light?

Review what you believe to be a limit to your life and work. Test it to see if it really is a limit. Prove yourself wrong.

What is the idea of you? The puzzle pieces that reveal a certain image projected onto the world? What is it about the idea of you that you want to change? What is it about the idea of your life or business that is asking for a fresh start?

We can imagine and then live the fiction of what could be. The way we create, build, and work are as unique as our own reflections. Leaning into someone else's frame to check our image against theirs sets up a comparison that assumes there is a race to be won, rather than a voice to be honed and heard. It assumes the grass is greener on the other side, or that it could be, and that thought is nothing more than a distraction.

exercise Sketching Your Ideal World

Get clear on what is the best of all possible worlds for you. Sketch it out, no matter how rough, in color on pages in your journal. One way to do this is to divide a two-page spread in your journal into thirds: morning, afternoon, and evening. Do some rough sketches in each third that represent the non-negotiables you want to do each day.

Maybe your morning section has a sketch of a yoga mat, a journal, a newspaper, or a quiet place to meditate. Underneath may be a sketch of you writing, speaking, or working with clients. Afternoon may hold images of lunch with a loved one, a walk, or a nap. Your evening section may show a quick drawing of a dinner table, a family meal.

In lieu of drawing, you may choose to find images in magazines or online that represent aspects of your ideal day and clients. Cut out and paste down your desired feeling states, ways of working, your highly defined client base, and how you would spend your days.

Imagine it all and live it now.

Becoming Indelible

I was in a trance as the train chugged toward Takaoka, Japan. The scene through the window looked like the many images I had seen on Japanese prints and porcelains. Mist hung on layered, verdant mountains with shrines, temples, and small homes dotting the steep hillsides.

Dad had his black-and-red buying-trip journal on his lap. He thumbed through the pages, studying the lists of the treasures he hoped to find on our adventure. He stopped at the section on bronzes, page after page of customer names alongside the designs they desired.

He closed the journal, looked up, and said, "We should be pulling into the station in about thirty minutes. You are in for an experience. Not every sixteen-year-old gets to see the epicenter of the lost-wax technique."

He grinned. I smiled right back. Dad knew I did not care one bit about how the bronzes were made. We also both knew that was going to change quickly. I was secretly very curious.

After all, I had typed hundreds of "lost-wax technique" stories onto tags for the bronzes we sold in his shop over several summers. Each tag had to be taped to the roller of his IBM Selectric typewriter, one at a time. One mistake, and I had to start over.

One afternoon, I said aloud in frustration, mimicking the story copy I was typing, "These damn tags are one-of-a-kinds."

Dad was walking by with an ikebana arrangement, overheard me, and chuckled. He sat the arrangement down and came over to me. He said:

> Let me explain to you the process of making these pieces. I think you'll find it interesting.
>
> The artisan starts with a clay model. He or she covers it with wax on which surface features of the image are carved. Clay is added to make an outer shell. The inner and outer shells are pinned together, and the entire mold is fired. The wax melts, runs out. Molten bronze is poured into the space created. When the bronze cools and hardens, the inner and outer shells are removed.
>
> This method produces items of exquisite detail and beauty. Each is a one of a kind. Like you.

He smiled at me, carefully lifted the arrangement, and walked to the front of the store to display the sparkling bronze container with its towering splay of flowers and line material.

While I did not enjoy typing those tags, the idea of being one of a kind certainly appealed to me. And ever since that summer afternoon in my teens, being one of a kind has been in the back of my mind. The quest to be original, indelible. Unable to be forgotten or replaced.

In seas of sameness, "red oceans of competition," the artistry of originality is one of the primary keys to success for every entrepreneur and creator. I believe we are all imprinted with a desire to stand apart from the crowd, letting the uniqueness of us, our vision, our creativity, cut through the din of the chattering, copycat masses. Many of us, though, are tempted to follow the market-leading pack, being careful to place our feet precisely in others' footprints, so that we can garner similar success.

Of course, the moment we do so, we are on the slippery slope to becoming a commodity in a crowded marketplace, competing on price.

How can we embark on the alchemical voyage of discovering, making, and sharing our own kind of music? How can we become the highly sought-after mold that will never exist again? How can we stand out in a crowd to be seen and remembered?

The happy news is that we already have everything we need for the journey. We are unique! We simply need to uncover our "lost wax" voices and visions, and then trust them.

exercise Revealing Your Unique Voice and Vision

A simple place to begin revealing our unique voice and vision is in our journals. Get a pen and begin writing down singular, delicious experiences you have had when you were made to feel extraordinarily special, profoundly connected.

Write down these details for each of the experiences you bring to mind:

- Where were you? Describe the environment.

- What were you doing? Describe the action and the players.

- Why did this experience move you so much?

- What is it that you value, appreciate, desire, or love that the experience resonated with?

- What clues does this experience offer you as to what may lead you to what you want to create?

I am willing to bet that as you worked on these answers, you experienced a burst of knowing. A flash of a memory. A sentence fragment from your soul. An image of something that sent electric shocks through your body.

Quickly, write down all the exclamations that bubble up. If you can sketch out or find pictures of any images you saw in your mind's eye, put them in your journal. Do not leave this work for later. It will evaporate, and you will not remember. Work it while the energy is popping and fresh.

· · · · ·

As entrepreneurs and creators, if we have the courage to deliver remarkable experiences, we will enjoy success that is buffered from the vagaries of market conditions, economic roller-coaster rides, and the advancing technological intelligence that threatens anyone whose work can be automated.

If we are willing to dig deeply for what brings us alive, we will be rewarded with the raw material for our creative expression, hints and bread crumbs for the path to becoming a category of one. The way to stand out in a crowd. A place of rare air, where we enjoy tapping the depths of us and making the whispers from our hearts real experiences in the lives of others. Such an intense and unbreakable connection with our ideal clients gives life to them *and* us, fostering our enduring success and impact.

Creating Your Future by Journaling

· ·

I was headed up the stairs in The Stone Lantern in July 1985. I was home from college on summer break, working at the shop. Dad stopped me as I was about to run to get a gift box for a package I was shipping out for a customer.

"I know how much you love paper," he said, smiling. "Do you want to see the journal I used when I first dreamed up The Stone Lantern?" He held out his small, brownish-red, ring-bound journal. I immediately knew how special, how important, that little vinyl book was.

As I leafed through it, he stood next to me, explaining its history and contents. "I started this when I was at the business school at Harvard," he said. "This notebook is where I mapped out each detail about the shop."

I read the pages, feeling the transfer of knowledge into my hands, traveling up to my shoulders, and exciting my heart before settling into my brain. Everything was in that book. Each detail of what he wanted to bring to life. He was passing a torch, a compendium of holy knowledge for my own journey.

When Hawaiians greet one another with "Aloha," they are sharing a sacred breath they believe is the creation of life. Dad sharing his journal with me was a profound aloha moment, breathing his incredible passion, wisdom, creativity, and thinking into me.

Decades later, when I was thinking through my idea for launching a real estate company during the Great Recession in 2010, I got a journal and started dreaming and recording each detail. I had to be precise, exceedingly thoughtful about each aspect, as I had scarce resources and one shot to get the plane into the air. Any forgotten detail could sink me.

I sat for hours and hours with my journal during the weeks around Christmas. We'd had a big snowstorm, and I was

"Get a notebook, Susie. You want one place to keep your ideas, think things through, and sketch out your vision. Write it all down."

Ralph deVille

grateful that my part of the world stood still during those planning days. I got clear on what I wanted to call into being, as well as on the precise details of the experience I wanted my firm to deliver.

I had no conscious recollection of the contents of Dad's journal, nor of his sage advice from twenty-five years before. I came to learn later how indelible his journal was, how it was as much a part of my DNA as his eyes and flat feet.

One afternoon, out of the blue, I had a flash of an image of that journal and the day at the foot of the stairs. I was immediately struck with a fierce zeal to find it. It had been over three years since Dad had died, and I wasn't sure if my brother-in-law, the manager of the shop, knew where Dad had kept it.

Jim pointed me toward a corner of boxes of Dad's photographs, papers, and memorabilia. I dug in. In the last box, covered in decades of dust and grime, I saw the journal.

When I picked it up, a shock of memories coursed through me. Snippets of our conversation, his smile, his explanations, his advice. Whoosh, whoosh, whoosh. I sat on the floor, surrounded by all his things, and collapsed forward as if I'd taken a blow to the gut. I cried until I could no longer breathe.

When I pulled myself together, I flipped back the cover and began reading. Lightning into each cell. The journal I had made in 2010 was an eerie mirror of the journal in my hands. My journal had almost identical sections and headings, including the same level of detail in my desired customer experience, pro forma statements, people to approach for advice, design of the office space, and logo and branding brainstorming.

Dad had even calculated how many sales he would need to make each hour, just as I had tried to nail down my minimum revenue. Our balancing beams between keeping a pulse in our businesses and folding had been only a couple of inches wide during our early years.

And then I got to the page with an image that made the room flip, front to back. I could not believe my eyes. How could this be?

Dad and I had never spoken about the specific inspiration for the design of the shop, or how he came upon the idea for the building's facade and display windows. As it turns out, a place that I hold sacred, Asilomar Hotel and Conference Grounds in Pacific Grove, California, had also grabbed his attention decades earlier.

I visited Asilomar after I left London, where I had been living for two years and working in the publishing industry, and was considering options for where I might live next. The Monterey area, with its stunning, rugged coastline and temperate climate, greatly appealed to me. From the moment I stepped onto the Asilomar grounds, I experienced the same sense of homecoming I'd had in Portugal. A part of me felt I had lived this moment before, that I somehow already knew this majestic place. It was a powerful connection that I could not explain.

Dad went on to create precisely what he had seen at Asilomar from his memories of being there. When I look at pictures of the complex and grounds today, I can see how the design influenced that of not only The Stone Lantern but also our family home, where I grew up and where my parents lived until 2014.

We have so much more power than we give ourselves credit for. Our ability to see what is not there and bring it into being is vast and often untapped. We can trudge along day to day without being cognizant that we are always creating our future reality, passively accepting what rolls in as our destiny.

I hope that by this point your journal is filled with all kinds of notes, sketches, messy ideas, inklings, crossed-out thoughts, and images. That you are willing to believe that journaling brings clarity to your thinking. That it connects and revs up the verbal and visual processing powers of your brain. I hope you notice that when your ideas are sketched out, it is easier to recognize gaps in your knowledge, as well as see connections and false assumptions.

I hope your journal becomes a great jumping-off point, helping you pinpoint ideas for deeper exploration. That it is a record of your evolving, thinking, and learning. I hope it helps you slow down, notice more, and develop deeper awareness that fuels informed, intentional action.

I hope that you will continue to use your journal each day and fill it up! Continue to engage with the life force within you—the sacred aloha breath of creation. Exhale onto the pages what you see and seek.

We are all fellow adventurers on this journey, holding our own maps as we try to find our desired destinations. What is True North for you? What do you aim for? What you are willing to declare and travel toward? Show us what you find along the way and any insider secrets or pitfalls. Lean into us for comfort, and we'll find inspiration in your vulnerability. Stand next to us at the foot of stairs. Show us how you transmit your dreams into reality. Breathe aloha into our lungs.

exercise Writing Multiple Passes

Many visual artists advocate having a "multiple passes" approach to doing their art. Recognizing that their painting, mixed media, or collage work gets infinitely more interesting with each pass and layer, they go to their canvas knowing that each time they begin, they will have something new to offer the piece. They won't be the same person as they were yesterday, so today's pass will lay down new energy, ideas, color, and design.

AJ Harper, author of *Write a Must-Read: Craft a Book That Changes Lives—Including Your Own*, advocates a multiple-pass approach when we edit our writing. Knowing that our brains cannot hold the details of a host of things to check in our manuscripts, we select one area of focus and go through the entirety of the work with that focus only. From this elevation, we can more clearly see where the gaps reside, what needs refining. Where we need to add stories and exercises. What we need to cut.

With this idea, go to your journal and start going through it in passes. Begin with one question or idea you would like to focus on, and then page through to see how your thinking and creativity have evolved. Next, go to the first blank page and begin writing where your thinking is today. What has survived? What has been reshaped? Where do you continue to have questions, doubts, or fears? What habits and rituals do you need to double down on, or remove? Where are you resisting making changes? What appears to be working above and beyond anything else? Why do you think that is the case?

You will be a different person tomorrow, so show up tomorrow and bring your new self to your art, your page. Capture the changes, the layers of who you are now and the future you that you are bringing into being. Notice the subtle differences in how you are incorporating what you are learning into your business and life. Continue to develop and add depth to this patina of your discoveries day by day. Dream up new destinations, fresh aspects of your desired future. Write it all down.

inspiration beacon

PURCHASE A small pack of four-by-six-inch index cards. At the top of one card, write "A.M. Rituals" and on another, write "P.M. Rituals." Think through the healthy habits and rituals you would like to put into place to bookend each day. Remember to add your 5MS to your A.M. Rituals card. Also, think through what you need to do each evening to set yourself up for success the next day.

Place your A.M. Rituals card on your desk or somewhere you will be sure to see it first thing each day. Place your P.M. Rituals card on your nightstand or near your bathroom mirror.

Experiment for a couple of weeks and see what impact these rituals have on your energy, clarity, sense of calm, focus, and creativity. Revise your cards as you see what works, what is missing, and/or what needs to be modified.

The Grand Adventure of Being You

"Make your mark on the world and leave a legacy worth aspiring to."

SIMON ASMUS

TUCKED INTO the high desert landscape of Galisteo, New Mexico, is the stunning Chi Center, a seventy-nine-acre complex for learning the ancient, energy-healing art of qigong. One border of the property is formed by massive blocks of bedrock, jutting toward the sky in squared-off, flat-surfaced chunks. During a retreat, the owner of the center shared with us that there were visible petroglyphs, carvings on the rocks, dating back to 5,000 BCE on the property. My friends and I excitedly hiked to the site to see for ourselves. We were not disappointed.

Native Americans have been leaving messages on rocks, or petroglyphs, for thousands of years. Like the art found in the caves of Eurasia dating back to 38,000 BCE, petroglyphs from different locations around the world are remarkably similar. Some theories suggest that they may have been a way of communicating with others or perhaps had a religious or ceremonial purpose. Regardless of their intended meaning or purpose, one cannot help but be immensely moved by studying the carvings.

As I ran my fingers across the boulders, feeling the carvings with my eyes closed, I imagined the person standing at that precise spot so many centuries before, tool in hand and message burning in their heart. There were images of animals, birds, lizards, and snakes, as well as symbols that appeared to depict people. But it was the carvings of human hands that took my breath away.

Like the Eurasian cave paintings made by early humans blowing pigment onto a hand held on a cave wall, the artists responsible for the carvings of hands into the bedrock said to me, "I was here. My life mattered."

The sun began to set, and my friends and I left the sacred site. Years later, the petroglyphs are still with me, prompting me to consider the compelling human desire to make a mark in the world. That is, to ensure that those who come after us are aware that we were here, and that our lives had meaning and impact.

The design and full living of one's life is, in my opinion, our most important and creative act of all. I wonder how often we are truly intentional about what it is we want to create each day, and if we are moving toward a greater vision of the legacy we want to leave. Or are we on some kind of automatic pilot in a distracted, numbed-out existence just "getting through the day"? Have we shelved the dreams that once called to us like sirens on a rocky shore?

Annie Dillard, author of *The Writing Life,* famously wrote, "How we spend our days is, of course, how we spend our lives." Will we wake up one morning and have the painful realization we have lived a life of days strung together by reaction, habit, and boredom? Or will we fully embrace the adventure of living our true nature, the one and only us? Can we find the courage to dig down under the layers of time, through the sediment of others' expectations and our own feelings of shortcomings and failure, to remember and retrieve what we came here to do and experience? To create what we, and only we, can create?

We are not unlike the early humans, filled with passion to convey to those who come after us that we once lived a life of meaning. How is it that you want to make your mark? What is it that you will create with what poet Mary Oliver calls your "one wild and precious life" that leaves a legacy of your highest intentions made manifest in the world?

exercise A Legacy

Take twenty minutes right now and write your answers to the following questions in your journal:

1   When I am gone, what is it that I want to survive me?

2   How might I invest in improving my present situation as well as in leaving something of substance behind for those in the future? Remember: We simply cannot know what will make others happy. But we can always know for ourselves.

Letting Go of Self-Improvement

"There's a paradox with self-improvement and it is this: the ultimate goal of all self-improvement is to reach the point where you no longer feel the need to improve yourself."
MARK MANSON

My great-aunt sat next to me in the back seat of the hearse. She dug a well-manicured thumbnail into the filter of her cigarette and said, "They should just go ahead and put me in the ground with her."

I looked out the window. I didn't know what to say.

Mom broke the silence. "I can't believe my mom is in the back of this car in a box!"

It was 1991, and the trees in Mount Zion Park Cemetery had begun dropping their spectacular autumn leaves. I watched them swirl and fall as we pulled away. I began to worry that I'd forget the details of Grandma's sweet face and voice.

Back at the house, I ducked into the bedroom where she had died. I sat on the edge of the bed and looked around the room. I touched the pillowcase, crisp from drying on the clothesline. I saw myself many years prior with my sister when we were probably seven and eight years old, running through sheets billowing on the line while Grandma pinned up socks, shirts, and pants.

I finally let myself cry.

This was my first experience with death, and I wanted no part of it. I rummaged through my bag and took out a book I had brought along to pass the time on the long drive from Highlands to Dayton. I hadn't even opened it once, but there in her room, I fell into it, relieved for the distraction.

This book would come to have an enormous influence on my life. It would change how I envisioned my future and ultimately lead me away from my life in London's publishing world and back to the mountains of North Carolina.

What Color Is Your Parachute? was my first self-help book, and I devoured each page and completed every exercise in it during my stay in Dayton. I jotted down notes in my prized leather Filofax, purchased at the stationer in Hampstead Heath. By week's end, I understood the essence of what brought me the most joy and had mapped out all I truly wanted in my life.

The detailed self-awareness and feeling of clarity of purpose pulled me right out of anxiety and sadness and filled me with an energy of optimism. My edgy knowing that I needed to change my life had lifted, and in its place was an empowered excitement for what came next.

In six months, I would be on a plane back to America and all of my belongings would be in a shipping container on the Atlantic Ocean, heading west. I became fixated on self-help and self-improvement. If I could get such a depth of understanding and direction from one book, what else was possible?

Cue the slippery slope, stage left.

I dove into self-help books of every stripe and subject matter. I figured that I could rebuild myself, repair my heart, and find a calling that enabled me to positively impact my community. All of that came true in profound and surprising ways. Even down to the smallest detail.

One morning, I stood on a chair with a screwdriver in my hand. I was adjusting the door in the former Highlands–Cashiers Hospital building, which I had helped convert into a community service center. A realization landed so hard, I almost fell off the chair: two years earlier, in my grandparents' living room, I had written down in my Filofax that I wanted to work in a charming old building as part of a team in service to my hometown. Of course, this reinforced my desire to dive even deeper. To saddle up for a long ride on the self-improvement horse.

Dig, dig, dig. Reflect, reflect, reflect. Heal. Create. All of which are positive and healthy activities. That is, until the once-innocent pursuit transformed into something else— *a subtle, gnawing way of thinking rooted in the belief that there was something about me that needed fixing.* And if you lift that rock, something creepy crawls out from underneath it: the thought that there's something inherently wrong with you.

Like all great paradoxes, the never-ending, relentless self-improvement quest has positive elements to it. After all, you do reap benefits and healthy change. Visible results. Goals

"The desire to improve
does not have to
come from a place of
self-loathing."

James Clear

reached. But is all that reaching toward something just a well-packaged denial of the understanding that we are mortal and flawed? What if we choose to believe we are already whole, already enough, already just fine, and already loved unconditionally?

I want to pause here and dive into this paradox more. First, let me reiterate that self-improvement does have a healthy place in our lives. The book you hold in your hands, after all, is not only a record of my own self-improvement journey but also inspiration for how you may experience the same. Our stance in how we approach this work on ourselves, though, is essential. We must be very clear on whether we are simply falling into the same old trap of trying to please others, if we are setting sail in an effort to race far away from feeling what we are feeling or being who we truly are.

In the Japanese animated fantasy film *Spirited Away*, a river spirit, covered in disgusting muck and grime, goes to a bathhouse. Mistaken for a stink spirit by the workers in the bathhouse, it is taken to a room to be cleaned.

The "stink spirit" was rotten with old stories, old expectations. The moment a bathhouse worker pulled the handlebar of an old bicycle wedged into its body, all the trash and ick of others that had attached to its being drained away, revealing a grand dragon-like spirit.

This river spirit is like the Golden Buddha that was once encased in concrete. Both the river spirit and the Golden Buddha are us once we unburden ourselves.

We can pursue self-improvement from the perception of having a purifying, herbal bath that removes all the trash that others have dumped into us. That we have dumped into ourselves. So rather than believing we have errors that need fixing, approach this work as a subtraction of all the stuff that is not us ... not the *true* us. That's the difference. And that's a key first step in bringing ourselves alive.

As you continue doing this work, know that we can have a balance of joyful becoming *while we love ourselves wholeheartedly right here, right now.* We can stretch ourselves from the confines of our comfort zones while knowing the new destination is a playful journey, not an effort to wring out flaws. We can find that a state of flow lands when we create right at the edge of what feels too hard without white-knuckle effort.

That is, as we do this work, we can hold two opposites in our mind simultaneously: We can release the seductive trap of pursuing endless self-improvement while we mindfully, intentionally create our new lives into being. We can hold the energy of an explorer, not that of a punisher looking to bleach out defects. We can know we are already whole, already just fine, while we wonder if we can open our hearts more and gently inspire the center of us with delight, color, and joy. We can jettison the urge to fix flaws and still reach the shores of our hearts' desires.

We can believe, maybe for the first time, our worth came along with our first breath, unearned. Delivered with divine and perfect love.

Watch for the evidence all around you that points to the creativity within you. Note, too, that what you have always considered your flaws are the kindling for the fire that only you can spark.

Asking for Help: How to Come to Terms with Disorder and Grief

"There's a lovely term in Irish, trína chéile, *which means everything's been turned upside down. The ability to let your experience turn upside down, to let yourself not know, to be* trína chéile *for a while, is very, very important."*
DAVID WHYTE

It had been a long three miles.

I got to the top of the second-to-last steep incline on my hike and stopped for a bit of rest. I could feel grief welling up from my chest and hitting my cheeks with tears. A light breeze stirred from the valley up to the ridge and rustled the trees. I lifted my head to catch it.

I realized I had spent the last mile walking as if I were trying to scale Mount Everest in a snowstorm, my oxygen dwindling. Head down, trudging forward, one laborious step after another.

I had no idea why I was so sad. The weight was an invisible, 150-pound pack upon my shoulders. Maybe the isolation of the last six months was catching up with me? Nah, I mindfully chose to embrace the solitude while sinking fully into long stretches of concentrated work and creative output. Was it worry or anxiety masquerading as sadness? Possibly. Frustration or anger? Possibly.

I knew enough to take an inner inventory to figure it out before I left the woods. I walked over to the edge of the trail and focused on a small waterfall formed by rain runoff. I let my gaze glaze over. Sophie darted in and out of the stream looking for a suitable stick. There was no sound other than the water splashes and the soft jingle of Sophie's name tag against her collar.

"This feels like a death of some kind," I said aloud. And then, "Oh... right. *Mine*."

For several years, I have been making a series of changes in my life. Many of those changes were reimagined, residual goals with progress that had stalled out or plateaued. I had chosen to recommit and tackle them anew.

Staring into the waterfall, I realized I was well on my way to accomplishing each of those life-changing goals. In fact, I was now near the finish line. My *kaizen* journey was not only within reach but also had already re-formed my identity.

Kaizen is a Japanese term that means continuous improvement via a gradual and methodical process. I like to think of it as the ability to change your entire life, one small step at a time.

As wonderful as it is, changing everything you want to change requires a dissolving of one's ego, the death of the old self. No matter how much pain we experience when we are stuck, this dissolving or dying part of the change process thrusts us into an odd and lonely grief that has a language that only our own inner voice speaks.

It is up to us to let ourselves die into our new selves.

I believe this dying into our new selves is what writer Joan Didion was referring to when she cited Yeats's poem "The Second Coming" and said, "The center cannot hold." She went on to say she felt "paralyzed by the conviction that writing was an irrelevant act, that the world as I had understood it no longer existed. It was the first time when I had dealt directly and flatly with the evidence of atomization ... the proof that things fall apart. If I was to work again at all, it would be necessary for me to come to terms with disorder."

We all have to come to terms with disorder, this atomization of the self, if we are going to stay the course. We must be willing to feel the grief all the way through and not succumb to pangs of retreat for comfort's sake.

When I feel all hope is lost, I know to turn my focus to what amazes and inspires me. The object of my attention can be the way water flows over mossy rocks along a trail in the woods, shadows playing on my desktop near my bay window, the first splash of paint mixed with water on paper, the sound of rustling wind in treetops, lines of poetry that lift me up and out of myself, the aroma of fresh bread in the oven, a work of art on the wall in my favorite museum, the sound of my son's voice on the phone, or the sight of Sophie smiling up at me from a swimming hole.

I now know that if I can sew together enough of these moments, I can cozy up inside their comfort and warmth and calm myself down. Ease the grip of fear. Take a deep breath and remind myself that I've been here before and can get through it again.

This connection to awe and a sense of wonder not only soothes and restores, but it also feeds the creative voice within me that has the same effect on others. In other words, when I connect to the Art of the World, I connect to the Art within Me and can help others connect to their own.

When we share what is our unique voice, our authentic nature, others look into the lens and feel a shudder of resonance in their bodies and hearts.

There is a gift in whatever is challenging for us. It is a reminder that what saves us is the experience of being alive. Not just visiting and being alive here on the surface, but also seeing, hearing, smelling, tasting, and feeling it all. Deeply.

Creativity begins a new conversation after the depth of our grief journey begins to ease and moves us forward. Irish poet, philosopher, and priest John O'Donohue said that an unseen life dreams us. I would add that our creativity dreams us into fully becoming. A cycle that repeats over and over throughout our lives, most especially as we are surfacing after experiencing profound pain and loss.

Creativity is our ladder up and out of the darkest caves of being. Each rung, each step, takes us closer to the center of who we truly are and opens the seams of darkness to let enough light fall at our feet.

Our instinct is to distract ourselves, buffer emotion, deaden the pain. But if we work the musculature of our grief, the tendons will loosen and give way to a softness that can support us. We work those muscles with pen, paper, color, paint, and our hands. Our hands engage in a healing circle with our brains and hearts.

If the specter of grief is in you now, I send you comfort and peace. Let us walk in fresh air together, even though we may be physically apart, and acknowledge where our grief journey is turning us, shaping us on the lathe of life experience. With each rotation, we can seek and find what soothes us most: the rich color that surrounds us and gently encourages us forward to make and meld colors of our very own. The colors that become the gift to ourselves now, and then to those who live on after us.

It is very odd that the journey of changing one's life for the better can feel really, really awful for most of the way. Even though we may be leaving the shore of a life that no longer serves us, the chaotic swirl sparked by our tiniest movement forward can make us feel intense motion sickness of the soul. And we don't want to ask for help.

That nausea can lie to us, elaborately, urging us to believe our second-guessing, those looks over our shoulders toward the life we are watching fade ever smaller into the distance. A system, a person, undergoing massive transformation must gradually decline into disorder for a certain period of time.

It feels impossibly heavy, toting the dead weight of our former self along with the next iteration of us.

We also have to take leave of our tendency, our allegiance, to crafting ourselves in the image of the concerns of others. We lower the emergency brake of how others want to shape us and press firmly down on the accelerator of our true self.

We are at what Joseph Campbell calls the threshold, on the cusp of transforming our consciousness. The moment we are about to embark into the outlying realms. Campbell counsels that we find our ultimate peace when we are "not compelled by desire or by fear, or by social commitments, when [we] hold [our] center and act out of there."

In these moments that feel surreal and impossible, with disorder as the norm, we entrepreneurs and creators can save the world by saving ourselves. We can spelunk our own depths for where we come alive and live accordingly, bringing the world to life in the process.

Ask for help. Don't walk past it. If you are intuiting that there's a resource, a basket of knowledge, or a mentor you need, stop and look around. This precious help is often right under our noses. Our tendency is to think we are somehow better off figuring it out on our own. We wrongly choose to wrestle with the cumbersome effort of going through it solo.

Look up the ladder to find the sherpa who is a few steps farther along than you. Someone who can still readily empathize with the tinge of being lost, but who has more dragon-slaying episodes under their belt than you. Find that person and ask for help.

This transformational process feels big because it *is* big! The right help, though, can help you pulverize chunks of the disorder you find yourself in, at the very moment you are dissolving and stretching into becoming the person you long to be.

Campbell says that the adventure we get is *the one we are ready for*. That it is a manifestation of our character.

We are ready.

Saying Yes to What Is Calling the Artist within You

"J'accepte la grande aventure d'être moi."
(I accept the grand adventure of being me.)
SIMONE DE BEAUVOIR

In the documentary on his life and work, *Nothing Changes: Art for Hank's Sake*, artist Hank Virgona sits at his desk in his studio in Union Square in New York City. He looks up at the camera and says that he comes into his studio every day in the hopes of making a discovery. And the discoveries are inexorably things he catches out of the corners of his eyes, little things he's done, he says, things he didn't realize he was even doing at the time. And that's what opens up new avenues to explore.

One of Hank's many unique talents was capturing the sense of a person through a spontaneous gesture, a very rapid sketch of a person he saw during his subway rides or walking past him on busy Manhattan streets. The sketches were often done in black ink on blank newsprint or on printed pages from books or newspapers. Later, back at his studio, Hank would use spot watercolor to further bring the small images to life.

Hank's colorful captures of an individual's essence take us to another understanding of what Lynda Barry refers to as images. In this instance, an image is the energy of who we are, netted like a butterfly by an artist, reflecting the outline of us to ourselves and others. Incredibly, we unknowingly reveal volumes about ourselves in a blink of an eye, through our posture, movement, and expression.

Hank was a master at bottling that lightning of the self, and in doing so, he felt connected to something unseen that filled him with a thrilling delight that removed pain from his then eighty-six-year-old body.

That bottled lightning of the self is precisely what we are on a voyage to discover for ourselves. We seek to know our lightning's depths, edges, and brilliance. To bring it to the surface with intention and turn up its intensity and authenticity.

Just as Hank was able to see and capture in three to four seconds a gesture that revealed insights of who a person genuinely was, so do our ideal clients see us. They "get us" that rapidly. They will connect with us, or not, in the blink of an eye. Are they making their decisions based on a mirage, a fabrication? Or are they seeing our true selves? Are they disengaging because there is nothing real or substantial that hooks into them, making them sit up and pay attention? Or are they stepping forward toward us because they intuit that we have done our work and share the same felt music, imagery, and driving passions?

Our adventure of becoming is seeing what others see in us, aligning what is true for us with who we are, while jettisoning what does not fit. This is our challenge. It is the foundation of a happy life, a successful business. The creation of programs, products, and services that the market needs and wants. When we become ourselves, we then lift up those we want to reach and impact. The energy you feel is the energy we feel. It connects, translates, and speaks to us.

Every transformational change we desire for the world requires sticky, resonant marketing that sparks people to do things differently. Pries them away from inertia through inspired action. The genesis of such resonant and persuasive marketing is the art of us. Without such a spigot driven into our bark, the sap will not flow from within us into the buckets of others. We fill bucket after bucket of change by becoming who we truly are, accessed through art and inspiration, shaping the ink of us into indelible images that generate unending influence and unstoppable reach.

What do you see out of the corners of your eyes? What stops you in your tracks and makes your insides flutter? What has the feeling of being "it" for you? That thing or person or moment or activity that connects you to something you cannot see? That takes pain from your body and your soul, just as it did for Hank?

Will you accept the grand adventure of being and living your true nature? Say yes to all that is calling to the artist within you. Say yes right now and never stop.

The ability to go on a Creative Rebel's Voyage is available to us in this moment. In any moment. And it is our ticket to living our grand adventure. We can rebel against the part of ourselves that wants to hide, not risk failure, not tolerate uncertainty. We can become like water and go around any obstacle while not losing our essential nature.

Our inability to tolerate uncertainty makes us frightened of our creativity. We worry that we don't know how to do it. That we don't know how our work, our voyage, is going to turn out. How good it will be. How successful it will be. Happily, none of those things matter!

What does matter is our *willingness*.

Look now at the pages in your journal. Flip through and take in all the words, sketches, ideas, and thoughts made by your willing hands. Unleashed by your courage to become visible and vulnerable in the doing. Do you feel the power of your willingness to try? The distance you have already traveled since we began?

Your journal is a steady and sure wind in your sails. It will always power you forward no matter the vessel, no matter the tide. It is your reliable nautical chart you create as you sail. Your safe harbor to take risks. It is your cauldron of inspired creating and the fire beneath the container, all in one. Our access point to the center of us and to where our creativity reserves reside—our back channels.

Our journal is where we can cast overboard the ballast that weighs us down and is not us: unhealthy habits, old expectations, anxiety over getting it wrong, staying stuck, losing love or favor. It is our lighthouse on the craggy shore, built and lit with our own hands, that guides us through any unforgiving night or relentless storm.

Most of us fear death, yet we spend a great deal of our time and energy avoiding truly living. For there is no vibrancy to life

"To be nobody-but-yourself—
in a world which is doing
its best, night and day,
to make you everybody else—
means to fight the
hardest battle which any
human being can fight."

e.e. cummings

without, as Dylan Thomas wrote, "the force that through the green fuse drives the flower." The force that is our creativity.

We are like an awe-inspiring Moroccan bazaar: if we let ourselves get lost among the colorful and seemingly impossible-to-navigate stalls, we can notice the colors, patterns, and textures of the fabrics that live on tightly bound rolls stashed inside of us. Bright, varied as countries, with their own languages and colors and music.

The decorum of truth-telling demands we abandon our carefully planned itineraries and leave them in a trash bin by the city's edge. We can learn that the map we've been following is a fool's errand. The hills that move farther away with our every advance are mirages built upon the sands of what everyone says we must do. There is no music or comfort there.

Let's all dig deep for what we truly want to represent us to those who need to hear it most. Don't turn your shoulders away and think the moment cannot be calling you. It is calling you.

We can choose to live fully, becoming and being a lighthouse. If we create from the true nature of us, our light will exist forever, reaching those we most want to impact, no matter the miles or millennia. As poet Diksha Suman said, "And some people never leave because their light still exists."

Trusting Yourself

. . . .

"Self-trust is the first secret of success."
RALPH WALDO EMERSON

There is nothing sexier than someone who is living in accordance with their true self.

Our ideal markets respond to the energy of us when we are seated firmly inside the skin of our core nature. Think of the times you have been shattered into a million pieces by something someone said, wrote, created, or lived that beautifully captured a zinging, piercing truth you have longed to express or experience with clarity and confidence.

We sense it coming before we even see or hear it. We are on alert. Our souls tip us off to sit up, pay attention, because here comes some straight-line power from the center of someone who is living in alignment and has zero concern for the opinions of others.

Isn't it interesting that no matter how many times we experience the allure and power of another's assured and authentic living, we will still slowly back up into the shrubbery and cloak what comprises that for us? We'll hide our truth not only from others but, painfully and deftly, from ourselves.

Why is it that we don't trust our own voices and hands and desires? I believe it is rooted in our obsession with not being judged harshly and our fear of losing favor, acceptance, and love. We'd rather die, withering in a desert of our own making, than risk our tender hearts by stepping into a supple, vibrant, and fully expressed life.

In a life of visible vulnerability, we attract attention and commentary. Commentary that can be brutal, mean, and pitted with jealousy.

As I work to shed these desires to hide in my own life and work, I begin the day by asking myself these questions: What choice do I have? On this one trip, this one adventure, this one life, who else am I supposed to be? I can only be myself, for better or worse.

Our time here is not meant to be spent making sure everyone else is comfortable with who we are, and our choices and decisions. All that second-guessing and worry over what others will think clouds our judgment. Decisions made from a mindset of lack or a concern of what we'll lose, especially favor and the approval of others, put us squarely in the Stagnation Zone when it comes to our creativity.

We all routinely forget that the inauthentic things we feel obligated to do or be not only are slowly and surely killing us and our joy, but also are daily exploding and splintering our opportunities for success.

Freedom begins in our inspired imagination and is animated when we leverage the bona fide essence of us with ease and determination. When we embrace what transports us to a lightness of being. When we live without apology or striving to feather out our rough edges to be more pleasing to the world. When we remember what it is we love and then dare to do it in broad daylight, uncompromising on our nonnegotiables for a passion-filled, ecstatic experience of this one life.

The breeze at dawn has secrets to tell you.
Don't go back to sleep.

You must ask for what you really want.
Don't go back to sleep.

People are going back and forth across the doorsill
where the two worlds touch.

The door is round and open.
Don't go back to sleep.

RUMI

Acknowledgments

I AM AWARE of how profoundly fortunate I am. I was born into an incredible family, winning both the parents' and the siblings' lotteries. My family formed the foundation of who I am, what I value, and how I see the world. They taught me the alchemical power of art, beauty, generosity, kindness, and being a good citizen and neighbor. They shaped my belief that I may somehow shape the world, make lasting contributions. Mom, Dad, John, and Anne, thank you for always being there for me and for your unwavering support. I love you from the depths of my being. Dad, I miss you so much. No words can hold or describe the loss of you. I feel your presence all around me and know you continue to cheer me on.

Adam, you have been my teacher from the moment I learned I was pregnant with you. You are the most genuine person I know, and your loving prods and questions always bring me home to my true self. Thank you for being my Buddha. To my stepchildren, Olen and Bevan, your courage to seek what brings you joy and fulfillment on your own terms inspires and reminds me to continue to do the same. I know the three of you will always reach the shores of your dreams if you keep searching, adventuring, and following your curiosity. I love you so very much and am enormously proud of you.

Publishing this book is the culmination of a lifelong dream. This journey has been one of a thousand surprises and learning experiences. I have joked with friends that writing this book was like being turned on a lathe, but in a good way. I welcomed this challenge, this stretching and becoming, and am incredibly grateful for all the talented, loving souls who helped me all along the way.

To Martha Beck, who plucked me out of the fires of my nuclear winter through the power of her life-coach training, writing, humor, and brilliance. Your coaching tools and guidance were the lifeline I desperately needed (I listened to *Steering by Starlight* no fewer than sixty times all the way through). I use what you taught me every single day in my work with clients and in the self-coaching work I do anytime I begin to believe a limiting thought.

To Pam Slim, who was able to hold space for me during a painful, frightening moment of decision in 2009. Through your masterful, profoundly loving coaching, I was able to see what I needed to change and how to surface the mettle to act. Our phone conversation served as a crucial point of departure and put me on the path to a new life. Fast-forward to 2022 and our work together on building out a certification program for my coaching framework: once again, your insights and guidance have been nothing short of spectacular.

To Fabienne Fredrickson, who first caught my attention in a video clip I came across on YouTube. I had just separated from my husband and was sitting up in bed surrounded by cardboard boxes. When I saw you onstage, speaking from your heart about the power of one's mindset, I thought, "She is absolutely who I need." I was right. You taught me how to rebuild my life and create systems of leverage in my business. You modeled joy, adventure, and vulnerability, which became my standard for the way I was determined to live.

To Jonathan Fields, whose mastery of curating loving, powerful community put me in a Soho loft for several days in 2016. Through your Art of Becoming Known experience, I was able to refine my coaching methodology and hone my messaging. When we worked together again a few years later, your coaching revealed to me even greater clarity about my target audience and how to reach them as well as key structural elements and copy for my web presence. You have an uncanny ability to blend the cerebral with soul and parse what is essential from noise.

To Knight Martorell, who was my sherpa as I ventured into the world of art-making and remembering how to see. What began as private sketching and watercolor lessons blossomed into one of my most treasured friendships. Knight, you not only guided me across the threshold of how to be more creative, you also gave me key counsel on how to approach the writing of this book. You took the time and effort to read my manuscript and offer suggestions for how to make it stronger, clearer. You were instrumental in the cover design process, helping me think through what it was I truly wanted, as well as offering several ideas of your own. You even drew the illustration (the elephant) for one of the key exercises in the book! Knight, you are a creative force with a heart of gold and an intellect that stuns.

To AJ Harper, who was my lantern in the darkness during the editing and revising phases of my book. You took the gloppy mess of my enormous first draft and "Edward Scissorhanded" your way through the deadwood. As a staunch voice of encouragement, you taught me how to write a must-read book that transforms the reader by always, always putting them first. You are a dear mentor and friend, and I am so indebted to you for all of your advice and advocacy.

To Elaine Holland, who was a fierce, strategic coach during a key time in my business and personal development. Thank you, Elaine, for letting me lean into your strength and experience and for bringing me back to getting leverage on myself to achieve absolutely anything I desired. You kept me focused on my "why" and on crafting the physical state required to make decisive actions and stay the course.

To Dr. Joe Dispenza, who taught me how to achieve heart-brain coherence through the power of meditation and how to harmonize the centers of my body. Through your books, lectures, and advanced weeklong retreat, I learned once and for all how to completely surrender to the unknown (and precisely how delicious that feels in the body). You showed me how to leverage the power I have to heal myself and the key habit of co-creating with the Unified Field.

To Mary Stacey, who brought a group of leaders to the rugged west coast of Ireland for a leadership and learning experience that was moving, poetic, and transformational. The week with you, David Whyte, Martin Hayes, and the outstanding circle of leaders from around the world reconnected me to my passion and vision, reminded me of the horizons that had called to me since birth, and grounded me into knowing the steps I had been too fearful to take.

To David Whyte, whose poetry inspires me to courageously live and create every day. Your words have been beacons for me for decades, but it was our time together in the Burren that chiseled off the concrete that had held me fast to a small life. On a chilly, misty day in August, you sat at Coleman's Bed, in the ancient limestone landscape in Ireland, and bore your eyes into mine, asking what decision I knew I had to make to leave the world of perceived safety and risk my heart in the most vulnerable way possible.

To Gail Larsen, who made indelible in my soul the notion that if we are to change the world, we must tell a better story. Through your Transformational Speaking Immersion in Santa Fe, you taught me how to articulate and serve others through my Original Medicine as well as the power of speaking from one's HomeZone. You refused to let me stay in my head, the scripted world, and instead pushed me right out of the nest to fly from my heart, where truth lands, resonates, and inspires. Your work and mentorship have forever changed me, and I deeply cherish our friendship.

To the incomparable Page Two team for your unparalleled service, support, creative insights, and love. From my first conversation with the soulful and sharp Trena White, I was hooked and knew that my book and its readers would be supremely well served by this group of outstanding professionals. I have never known such a circle of dedicated and talented publishing stars. Special thanks to my editors, Amanda Lewis and Scott Steedman, who, with humor and skill, painstakingly edited this book and made it the best it could possibly be. I also offer my deepest appreciation to the design team, Taysia Louie and Peter Cocking, for their creativity and boundless patience as we worked together to create a showstopper of a book cover.

To Rachel Gogos, who has been a confidante and trusted advisor since I met her in a Soho loft (thank you, Jonathan Fields!). You have helped me shape and craft my online presence, growing and changing with me as I came into my own with greater clarity and confidence. You amplify what is the best in others and connect us with those we dream of serving. Thank you, too, for reading my manuscript and giving me your suggestions and key input. Our friendship is a source of strength and joy.

To Donna Cravotta, who told me from the beginning that one births a book, and to take my time. You guided me toward marketing and branding essentials when I was on my knees, groping around in the dark. Your wizardry with language revealed the spot-on name for my coaching methodology, the Creative Rebel's Voyage. Our work together gave me structure for my thinking and voice to my vision. You are my "May 1st sister" in every sense of the word.

To Susan Hyatt, who models standing in one's truth with pluck and moxie. The question you posed over dinner one night in Dundas Castle cracked away the fear I had been holding over devoting myself to writing and creating without limit. Your humor and unapologetic stance are infectious and your willingness to create what you crave ripples throughout the world.

To Gabi Dalnekoff, Susan M. Barber, Lori Petersen, and Cyndi Thomason, who took on the enormous task of being peer reviewers of my manuscript. The moment I asked for your help, you all jumped in and took the time to carefully read the entire book. Your thoughtful suggestions and feedback shaped this book and its impact.

To my sweet friends scattered all over the world, I love you. Know you reside in my heart and that there is a piece of you in this book.

Recommendations

I AM DELIGHTED to recommend the following professionals, who are all uniquely gifted in their fields of expertise. As I mentioned in the acknowledgments, each was an essential supporter during my own Creative Rebel's Voyage.

· ·

AJ Harper is a developmental editor and publishing strategist who helps authors craft must-read books people love, rave about, and keep forever. She is the author of *Write a Must-Read: Craft a Book That Changes Lives—Including Your Own.*

AJHarper.com

· ·

Cyndi Thomason is an entrepreneur, author, and speaker. She is passionate about helping business owners create businesses that work to support them and their families. Her first book, *Profit First for Ecommerce Sellers*, helps ecommerce business owners create a permanently profitable business. Her latest book, *Motherhood, Apple Pie, and All That Happy Horseshit*, guides new or expecting moms through the journey of establishing a successful business. Cyndi also founded and is the president of bookskeep, one of the early accounting firms to begin serving ecommerce businesses.

CyndiThomason.com and bookskeep.com

. . . .

David Whyte is an internationally renowned poet, author, and speaker. He is the author of ten books of poetry; three books of prose on the transformative nature of work; a widely acclaimed, bestselling book of essays; and an extensive audio collection.

DavidWhyte.com

. . . .

Donna Cravotta is the CEO and founder of Cravotta Media Group, a small unagency intentionally designed to build media platforms for content creators and small to mid-sized businesses. Donna and her team listen first, work collaboratively, and leverage content to build a meaningful online presence that connects with the right people to make a bigger impact.

CravottaMediaGroup.com

. . . .

Elaine Holland is director of coaching, Robbins Research International, Inc.

TonyRobbins.com

. . . .

Fabienne Fredrickson is the founder of the Boldheart Business program, which guides entrepreneurial women to multiple six and seven figures in their business, with fourteen to sixteen weeks of unplugged vacation per year. It's all based on the concept of leverage. To start your journey, Fabienne invites you to read her book *The Leveraged Business: How You Can Go from Overwhelmed at Six Figures to Seven Figures (and Gain Your Life Back)*.

Boldheart.com

. . . .

Gabi Dalnekoff is the CEO and founder of AweVida, a real estate investment company that inspires others by openly sharing powerful life lessons in a home renovation setting.

AweVida.com

. . . .

Gail Larsen is a teacher and the author of *Transformational Speaking: If You Want to Change the World, Tell a Better Story*. *Fast Company* describes Gail's work as "transforming your relationship to your voice via the deepest stirrings of your soul." Her original process for finding and speaking your truth to open hearts and inspire change serves change artists across the globe and includes four members of Oprah's Super Soul 100.

RealSpeaking.com and TransformationalSpeakingOnline.com

. . . .

Dr. Joe Dispenza holds a bachelor of science degree and is a doctor of chiropractic. His post-graduate training includes the fields of neuroscience and neuroplasticity, quantitative electroencephalogram (qEEG) measurements, epigenetics, mind–body medicine, and brain/heart coherence. As a researcher, lecturer, author, and corporate consultant, he is interested in demystifying the mystical so that people have all the tools within their reach to make measurable changes in their lives.

DrJoeDispenza.com

Jonathan Fields is the founder of Good Life Project® and Spark Endeavors. He is a dad, husband, award-winning author, executive producer, and host of one of the top-ranked podcasts in the world, *Good Life Project*. He is also the founder of a series of companies focused on human potential, and is currently helming Spark Endeavors, where he developed the groundbreaking Sparketype® Assessment. His latest book, *Sparked: Discover Your Unique Imprint for Work That Makes You Come Alive*, is both a rallying cry and a field guide to reclaiming work as a source of meaning, joy, and possibility.

GoodLifeProject.com and Sparketype.com

Knight Martorell, a true Renaissance man, is an architect, artist and illustrator, designer, musician, and all-around great human. Although he works fluently in any medium, Knight specializes in watercolor, pen, and Prismacolor.

MartorellStudios.com

Lori Petersen is the CEO and founder of AccountSolve, which helps small businesses in the interior design space be in command of their money. AccountSolve uses proven systems and processes to guide clients toward streamlined money management and higher profitability.

Account-Solve.com

Martha Beck is a *New York Times*–bestselling author and life coach. She is a Harvard-trained sociologist and the creative visionary behind Wayfinder Life Coach Training and many other programs. The discovery of Martha's work is often a moment of relief and excitement for Wayfinders, as they finally discover language for what has felt different about them.

MarthaBeck.com

. . . .

Mary Stacey is the founder of Context Consulting and Burren Executive Leadership Retreat. The Burren retreat is an annual gathering in Ireland at the intersection of artistic and leadership practice; it interweaves peer leadership conversations, creative process, and landscape learning in support of each participant's leadership growth, and a fresh collective view of what leadership can be for the twenty-first century.

ContextConsulting.com and BurrenLeadership.org

. . . .

Page Two is an innovative publishing company that offers authors a faster path to market, more creative control, and deep engagement in their launch strategy. The cofounders, Jesse Finkelstein and Trena White, have a combined forty years of experience in the industry. They launched Page Two in 2013 to help thought leaders, subject matter experts, and organizations publish leading non-fiction books.

PageTwo.com

. . . .

Pamela Slim, CEO and cofounder of K'é Main Street Learning Lab, is an award-winning author, speaker, and business coach who works with small business owners ready to scale their businesses and IP. She is the author of *Escape from Cubicle Nation*, *Body of Work*, and *The Widest Net*. Pam and her husband, Darryl, cofounded the K'é Main Street Learning Lab in

Mesa, Arizona, where they host scores of diverse community leaders and regular small business programming.

PamelaSlim.com

. . . .

Rachel Gogos is the founder and CEO of brandiD, a soulful digital agency that builds online platforms for leaders and experts so they can profit with purpose. A savvy team of strategists, copywriters, designers, and developers, brandiD helps clients amplify their voices in a way that gets them noticed through a one-of-a-kind web presence.

ThebrandiD.com

. . . .

Susan M. Barber is an author and the president of Susan M. Barber Coaching & Consulting. A former Fortune 500 IT director, Susan is an executive coach focused on helping business leaders play bigger and increase their visibility so they can elevate their position in the workplace. As the author of *The Visibility Factor*, she is creating a movement that enables leaders to highlight their value and leadership strengths as well as be seen for their true talent.

SusanMBarber.com

. . . .

Susan Hyatt is the CEO of Susan Hyatt, Inc., and founder of The University for Life Coach Training. Susan is a master certified life and business coach, bestselling author, TEDX speaker, and the queen of helping women create what they crave in life. Her number one passion is helping women get more of whatever they want—money, confidence, energy, joy.

SHyatt.com and UniversityforLifeCoachTraining.com

Notes

Chapter 1: Breaking Free

p. 22   *used my body as a transport mechanism for my head*: Sir Ken Robinson, "Do Schools Kill Creativity?" TED, February 2006, video, 19:12, ted.com/talks/sir_ken_robinson_do_schools_kill _creativity/transcript.

p. 25   *as told in the captivating film* Finding Joe: *Finding Joe*, directed by Patrick Takaya Solomon (2011; Pat and Pat Productions, 2012), DVD.

p. 34   *Voltaire advocated in his novella* Candide: Voltaire, *Candide, or Optimism*, trans. Theo Cuffe (New York: Penguin, 2005). Originally published in 1759.

p. 37   Merriam-Webster *defines agency as*: *Merriam-Webster*, s.v. "agency (*n.*)," merriam-webster.com/dictionary/agency.

p. 38   *what inspiration is and the power it holds over our destinies*: Paulo Coelho, "Paulo Coelho on Inspiration," Be the Change, streamed December 19, 2016, YouTube video, 2:50, youtube.com/watch? v=x0Rh10ylO-s.

Chapter 2: Opening Up to Inspiration

p. 50   *you, too, have most likely been art-shamed*: "Brené Brown on 'Big Strong Magic,'" in *Magic Lessons*, hosted by Elizabeth Gilbert, July 25, 2016, podcast, season 1, episode 12, 35:22, elizabeth gilbert.com/magic-lessons.

p. 63   *three pages written in longhand each day*: Julia Cameron, *The Artist's Way: A Spiritual Path to Higher Creativity* (Los Angeles, CA: JP Tarcher/Putnam, 2002).

p. 76　*He would later describe these five years as*: Joseph Campbell, *Joseph Campbell: The Hero's Journey* (Novato, CA: New World Library, 1990), 52.

p. 78　*Cal Newport calls "deep work"*: Cal Newport, *Deep Work: Rules for Focused Success in a Distracted World* (New York, NY: Grand Central Publishing, 2016).

Chapter 3: Accessing Your Creativity
Back Channels (By Bringing Yourself Alive)

p. 83　*what Lynda calls "back of mind"*: "Lynda Barry: Accessing the Imaginary," UM Stamps, streamed October 7, 2013, YouTube video, 57:26, youtube.com/watch?v=x5QsOg-7B6w.

p. 87　*a drawing exercise inspired by art teacher Betty Edwards*: Betty Edwards, *Drawing on the Right Side of the Brain*, 4th ed. (New York, NY: TarcherPerigee, 2012).

p. 90　*Author Sam Anderson describes the process this way*: Sam Anderson, "Letter of Recommendation: Blind Contour Drawing," *New York Times* magazine, May 17, 2015, nytimes.com/2015/05/17/maga zine/letter-of-recommendation-blind-contour-drawing.html.

p. 94　*Amanda celebrated her milestone in a Facebook post*: Amanda Palmer, Facebook, December 26, 2019, facebook.com/amanda palmer/photos/a.10151728148973375/10157271269848375.

p. 97　*Artist Ralph Steadman says*: D'Arcy Doran, "Ralph Steadman, Gonzo Artist: SXSW Field Notes," *Huck*, March 9, 2014, huckmag .com/art-and-culture/art-2/ralph-steadman-gonzo-artist.

p. 102　*Lynda Barry touches upon this*: "*Design Matters* with Debbie Millman: Lynda Barry," *Design Matters*, October 28, 2019, Sound-Cloud, MP3, 52:25, soundcloud.com/designmatters/design-matters-with-debbie-millman-lynda-barry.

p. 103　*gifted her with startling advice*: Ibid.

p. 112　*Steven Pressfield calls one's Resistance*: Steven Pressfield, *The War of Art: Break Through the Blocks and Win Your Inner Creative Battles*, 16th ed. (New York, NY: Black Irish Entertainment, 2012).

p. 112　*what Pressfield describes as "precious" status*: Ibid.

p. 116　*worded by Irish poet John Anster*: This couplet was part of Anster's 1835 "free and poetical" translation of Johann Wolfgang von Goethe's *Faust*. See quoteinvestigator.com/2016/02/09/boldness.

p. 117　*study yourself like a researcher would study a bug*: "*The Tim Ferriss Show* Transcripts: Jim Collins (#361)," *The Tim Ferriss Show*,

February 20, 2019, podcast, episode 361, 2:22:21, tim.blog/2019/
02/20/the-tim-ferriss-show-transcripts-jim-collins-361.

p. 124 *fine-tune your philosophy from there*: Feel free to email it to me at
info@InnovationandCreativityInstitute.com (with "My Personal
Philosophy" in the subject line) for feedback!

Chapter 4: Putting Your True Self Back at the Helm

p. 129 *the conversational nature of reality*: "David Whyte: The Conversational Nature of Reality," *On Being with Krista Tippett*,
April 7, 2016, podcast, 51:39, transcript updated December 12,
2019, onbeing.org/programs/david-whyte-the-conversational-
nature-of-reality/.

p. 129 *In the film* Adaptation: *Adaptation*, directed by Spike Jonze (2002;
Culver City, CA: Sony Pictures Home Entertainment, 2003), DVD.

p. 130 *As Kaufman notes*: You can find the entire transcript of Kaufman's
talk here: BAFTA, "Screenwriters' Lecture: Charlie Kaufman,"
September 30, 2011, bafta.org/media-centre/transcripts/
screenwriters-lecture-charlie-kaufman transcript.

p. 133 *one of the design leads in the video said*: You can watch the entire
video here: ABC News *Nightline*, "IDEO Shopping Cart Design
Process," June 13, 1999, YouTube video posted by Davit
Sahakyan, September 29, 2017, 22:02, youtube.com/
watch?v=izjhx17NuSE.

p. 139 *Lamott cautions us*: Anne Lamott, *Bird by Bird: Some Instructions
on Writing and Life* (New York, NY: Anchor, 1995), 28.

p. 140 *As Glass points out*: "Ira Glass on Storytelling 3," posted by
warphotography, July 11, 2009, YouTube video, 5:20, youtube
.com/watch?v=X2wLPoizeJE.

p. 141 *to rebel against social pressures*: Ray Bradbury, *Zen in the Art of
Writing: Essays on Creativity*, 3rd ed., expanded (Santa Barbara,
CA: Joshua Odell Editions, 1993).

p. 142 *an exercise similar to this over thirty years ago*: Richard N. Bolles,
*What Color Is Your Parachute? A Practical Manual for Job-Hunters
and Career-Changers*, rev. ed. (Berkeley, CA: Ten Speed Press, 2020).

p. 143 *Author Martha Beck cautions us*: Martha Beck, *Finding Your Own
North Star: Claiming the Life You Were Meant to Live* (New York, NY:
Harmony, 2002).

p. 146 *reconnecting with our "elemental waters"*: David Whyte, *Crossing the
Unknown Sea: Work as a Pilgrimage of Identity* (New York, NY:
Riverhead, 2002).

p. 148   *ask himself one powerful question*: Austin Kleon, "What Did
You Really Want to Say?" *Austin Kleon* (blog), August 1, 2020,
austinkleon.com/2020/08/01/what-did-you-really-want-
to-say-2.

p. 149   *Brian Koppelman presented himself*: "*The Tim Ferriss Show*
Transcripts: Brian Koppelman on Making Art, Francis Ford
Coppola, Building Momentum, and More (#424)," *The Tim Ferriss
Show*, May 14, 2020, podcast, episode 424, 1:30:36, tim.blog
/2020/05/14/brian-koppelman-transcript/.

p. 150   *In a documentary on the comedian*: *Joan Rivers: A Piece of Work*,
directed by Ricki Stern and Annie Sundberg (2010; Montreal:
Seville Pictures, 2013), DVD.

p. 151   *Author and researcher Joe Dispenza calls this*: Dr. Joe Dispenza,
"You Already Know How to Do This," *Unlimited: Dr. Joe Dispenza*
(blog), December 12, 2020, drjoedispenza.com/blogs/dr-joes-
blog/you-already-know-how-to-do-this.

p. 152   *author and academic Verlyn Klinkenborg asserts*: Verlyn Klinkenborg,
Several Short Sentences about Writing (New York, NY: Vintage,
2013), 37.

p. 152   *Klinkenborg suggests that we do this by*: Ibid.

Chapter 6: The Provenance of Becoming

p. 190   *Colbert decided to dig deep and go off script*: Brian Steinberg, "CBS,
Stephen Colbert Plot Live 'Late Show' following Trump State
of the Union," *Variety*, January 11, 2018, variety.com/2018/tv/
news/cbs-stephen-colbert-live-late-show-trump-state-of-the-
union-1202661127.

p. 191   *David Whyte reminds us*: "David Whyte: The Conversational
Nature of Reality."

p. 197   *The MoMA website explains*: *The Artist Is Present*, Marina Abramović,
MoMA Learning, moma.org/learn/moma_learning/marina-
abramovic-marina-abramovic-the-artist-is-present-2010.

p. 200   *As Brené Brown notes*: Brené Brown, "The Power of Vulnerability,"
TEDxHouston, June 2010, video, 20:03, ted.com/talks/
brene_brown_the_power_of_vulnerability.

p. 208   *The iconic music denoting the approaching shark*: *Jaws: The Inside
Story*, directed by Georgia Manukas (2010; Biography Channel,
TV movie, documentary).

Chapter 7: The Artist and the Entrepreneur

p. 235 *advocates a multiple-pass approach*: AJ Harper, *Write a Must-Read: Craft a Book That Changes Lives—Including Your Own* (Vancouver: Page Two, 2022).

Chapter 8: The Grand Adventure of Being You

p. 240 *Annie Dillard, author of* The Writing Life: Annie Dillard, *The Writing Life* (New York, NY: Harper Perennial, 2013).

p. 241 *what poet Mary Oliver calls*: Mary Oliver, "The Summer Day," in *House of Light* (Boston, MA: Beacon Press, 1992).

p. 242 *was my first self-help book*: Bolles, *What Color Is Your Parachute?*

p. 245 *Japanese animated fantasy film* Spirited Away: *Spirited Away*, written and directed by Hayao Miyazaki (Japanese); English version directed by Kirk Wise (2001; Walt Disney Studios Home Entertainment, 2015), Blu-ray.

p. 248 *what writer Joan Didion was referring to*: Joan Didion, *Slouching towards Bethlehem* (New York, NY: Farrar, Straus and Giroux, 2008), preface.

p. 249 *John O'Donohue said that*: John O'Donohue, *Anam Cara: A Book of Celtic Wisdom* (New York, NY: Harper Perennial, 1998).

p. 250 *Campbell counsels that we find our ultimate peace when*: "Joseph Campbell and the Power of Myth: 'The Hero's Adventure,'" BillMoyers.com, episode 1, June 28, 1988, transcript, billmoyers .com/content/ep-1-joseph-campbell-and-the-power-of-myth-the-hero%E2%80%99s-adventure-audio.

p. 251 *Campbell says that the adventure we get*: Ibid.

p. 251 *In the documentary on his life and work*: *Nothing Changes: Art for Hank's Sake*, directed by Matthew Kaplowitz (2018; New York, NY: Burning Hammer Productions).

p. 256 *as Dylan Thomas wrote*: Thomas's titular poem can be found at Poets.org, poets.org/poem/force-through-green-fuse-drives-flower.

p. 256 *As poet Diksha Suman said*: Diksha Suman (@beingsheblog), Instagram post, July 25, 2020, instagram.com/p/CDEcdwvl3gO.

p. 258 *The breeze at dawn has secrets to tell you*: Rumi, "The Breeze at Dawn," in *The Essential Rumi*, expanded ed., trans. Coleman Barks (New York, NY: HarperOne, 2004).

Thank You

THANK YOU so much for reading this book and for being willing to go on this adventure with me. I sincerely hope you have enjoyed your experience and are walking away with fresh insight and tools to propel you forward. Take a moment and recognize how far you've already come, what you've already accomplished, the hardships you have overcome. Keep going. You absolutely have what it takes to find the freedom and success you crave.

I imagine your journal is filled with inspiring notes, images, sketches, and ideas! Please keep your journaling practice going. If you'd like to share some of your journal pages, please post them on the social platforms of your choice with the hashtag #BuoyantBook.

How May I Support You in Your Wild Season of Becoming?

R EGARDLESS OF WHERE we are on our journey—whether we are just starting out or have years of experience on the entrepreneurial path—often, we need inspiration, coaching, accountability, and community to help us make significant progress, especially when we are stuck and unclear.

At the Innovation & Creativity Institute, I offer multiple ways you can get the key help you need, delivered in the way that suits you best. I would love to support you through one or more of the following:

Join the *Inspired!* Community

Sign up at InnovationandCreativityInstitute.com for my free, weekly newsletter, *Inspired!*, for lessons and tips to help you navigate your Creative Rebel's Voyage.

Private Coaching and VIP Days

Reignite your creativity, energy, and agency with one-on-one entrepreneurial coaching and VIP experiences designed to help you explode areas of stuckness and enjoy exponential growth.

The Sketchbook Entrepreneur Masterclass

Access your creativity and move into freedom in this live, online six-week masterclass that will take you on an archeological dig of the self so you can reveal and reclaim your inspired creativity and strategic mindset.

The Buoyant Way Certification Program

The Buoyant Way is an immersive training and certification program and retreat for coaches, consultants, and advocates of social change. The work is based on the groundbreaking Creative Rebel's Voyage methodology.

Speaking at Your Event

I would love to join you for fireside chats, keynotes, Zoom gatherings, workshops and/or seminars, or be a guest presenter at your next retreat. I promise to make our time together engaging, action-packed, fun, powerful, and transformational.

Copies for Your Organization

If you'd like to purchase multiple copies of *Buoyant* for your team, event, or to give as gifts, please contact me at **orders@InnovationandCreativityInstitute.com**. Discounts may be available, based on volume.

A Favor

I could use your help! If you have gotten value from this book and would like to share your thoughts, would you take a minute or two to please write a review? I would really appreciate it! Reviews from readers like you are enormously meaningful for the book's success, reach, and impact.

Let's Start the Conversation

Send me an email or reach out via one of the social platforms below to ask me questions and/or discuss ways I may be of service to you. I'm looking forward to hearing from you.

✉ info@InnovationandCreativityInstitute.com

🌐 InnovationandCreativityInstitute.com

🅕 susie.deVille

🅞 @susie_deVille

🅛 susiedeVille

🐦 @susiedeVille

CHELSEA SANDERS

About the Author

SUSIE DEVILLE is dedicated to helping entrepreneurs build wildly successful businesses by rediscovering their creativity and leveraging the power of their true nature. An author, coach, and entrepreneur who built and sold a highly profitable real estate firm, Susie has been researching innovation and creativity since 2005, using her findings to create her signature methodology, the Creative Rebel's Voyage. She is the founder and CEO of the Innovation & Creativity Institute, and trained as a coach with Dr. Martha Beck. She lives in the mountains of Highlands, North Carolina, with her golden retriever, Sophie.

InnovationandCreativityInstitute.com